Organizations:
An Information
Systems Perspective

Kenneth E. Knight
University of Texas at Austin

Reuben R. McDaniel, Jr.
University of Texas at Austin

Wadsworth Publishing Company, Inc.
Belmont, California

Management Editor: John Mahaney
Production Editor: Anne Kelly
Designer: Cynthia Bassett
Copy Editor: Paul Monsour
Technical Illustrator: Lori Gilbo

Printed in the United States of America

1 2 3 4 5 6 7 8 9 10—83 82 81 80 79

Library of Congress Cataloging in Publication Data
Knight, Kenneth.
  Organizations.
  Bibliography: p.
  Includes index.
  1. Organization. 2. Organizational behavior.
3. Information theory. 4. Systems theory.
I. McDaniel, Reuben R., joint author. II. Title.
HD31.K564   301.18′32   78-8929
ISBN 0-534-00583-7

To Ann and Myra
who organize the world for
Diane, Heather, Jennifer, K.C.,
Reuben, and so many others

Contents

7   Organizational Response to Complexity   109

8   Organizations as Process-Following, Problem-Solving, and Decision-Making Systems   121

9   The Organization as an Evolving System   147

Preface

Organizational theory has become increasingly important, and past literature and research provide a significant body of knowledge for us to draw upon. This book attempts to construct a consistent framework for a portion of this body of knowledge. The development of the framework is based on information and systems concepts applied to organizations. We use a systems-information approach to describe the flow of information and its transformation by organizational systems. In developing this perspective to organizational theory, we have carefully explained the concepts necessary to describe organizations and their behavior in terms of information flows, information transformations, and systems analysis.

Because information flows in an organization are dynamic, organizations must be described using a perspective that develops an understanding of the dynamics of any situation. The systems perspective provides a means for such understanding. Systems analysis enables us to examine the separate elements or subsystems and the interactions between the elements.

The information systems perspective is unique in using information, information flows, and information processing as the key variables to describe organizations. Organizational structure consists of the content and directions of standard information flows, task distribution, and the interactions between the information processors in an organization. There is no simple internal logic that dictates proper organizational structure. The design and management of an organization are related to the nature of the critical information flows—thus, the form and the function of an organization are directly related. We have oriented this text toward helping the reader understand how to determine the critical information, information flows, and information processing of an organization. If the critical information flows are relatively certain and stable over time, the organization is likely to be characterized by a high level of routine in structure and behavior. However, if the critical information flows are relatively uncertain and unstable over time, the organization is likely to have a large number of nonroutine functions creating variability in both structure and behavior.

We have selected an information systems perspective because it is a practical and effective way to describe organizations. It provides a useful framework for students of organizational theory, designers of organizations, and managers of organizations. It can also help each of us who are involved with and interact with organizations during much of our waking lives.

For brevity and simplicity, we have not reviewed the published research and literature in detail. We have tried to develop a framework that allows us to study complex concepts in nonmathematical terms. The first seven chapters of this book present the basic systems concepts and express organizational theory concepts in information and systems terms. We start with the basic concepts of information, information processing, information selection and distortion, and systems theory, and conclude with a discussion of complex systems. The final three chapters use systems terms to describe the basic functions performed by organizations.

We have written this book for both advanced undergraduates and graduate students. The consistent framework the book offers should make it valuable as a basic text or as a supplement in courses on organizations, management, organizational behavior, and business policy.

We owe a great deal to all the scholars who have written about organizations and contributed so much to this textbook. For her direct support, we are most indebted to Helen Baca who assisted us with the many revisions over the past years and made invaluable editorial contributions. We also acknowledge the cooperation of the thousands of University of Texas College of Business Administration students who used earlier drafts of the text and offered their evaluation of it. While we were working on the manuscript, our colleagues also actively contributed to its development. We particularly thank Doug Engle, Jim Glenn, Larry Foster, Bill Swanson, Wayne Donnelly, and Shirley Gamble. Finally, we are grateful to those reviewers who made helpful comments on the manuscript: Patrick E. Connor, Oregon State University; John C. Henderson, Ohio State University; Robert J. Keller, University of Houston; Stephen R. Michael, University of Massachusetts; H. Joseph Reitz, University of Florida; and J.B. Ritchie, Brigham Young University.

While our debts to all our colleagues are immeasurable, we take full responsibility for the final product. Trying to provide a consistent framework for an extremely disjointed field is not without risks. We obviously felt these risks were worth taking, and we have found the project extremely enjoyable and rewarding.

Organizations and Information

1

Introduction

Organizations are increasingly important in modern society. While family and friendship groups continue to play large roles in our lives, formal organizations are the mechanisms chosen for dealing with many problems: Nursing homes take care of aged relatives; public schools educate children; labor unions negotiate wages; insurance companies pay survivors. The complexity of living is such that to function effectively without formal organizations would be difficult. There is considerable evidence that in the future, society will increasingly rely on organizations to deal with problems.[1]

Organizations are often viewed as faceless creations of an uncaring culture. The bureaucracy has come to represent rules, regulations, and restrictions. Despite feelings of helplessness *without* organizations, there are often feelings of helplessness with them; it seems as if nothing can be accomplished because organizations are in the way. At the same time, many things can only be accomplished through organizations because they have the necessary resources and power. The result often is a love-hate relationship with formal organizations. Emotion rather than reason dictates responses to the demands of highly organized society.

Despite the fact that organizations play such a pervasive role in society, little is known about their nature. Most people have some vague notions about organizational structure. People usually feel that if organizations were effectively and efficiently managed, everyone would be better off. Some relationship between structure and management is occasionally con-

1

sidered. This book will answer some questions about the nature and structure of organizations and about the management of organizations. Through this understanding the organizational world may seem less contradictory, less capricious, more understandable, and more manageable.

Focus on Information

Many perspectives on organizations attempt to define one best way for structuring and managing. The assumption is made that there is an internal logic in the design of organizations that dictates form independently of function and that leads to certain optimal principles of management. A combination of the correct organizational form and adherence to the principles of management will produce efficiency and effectiveness. The perspective used in this book is different: There is no simple internal logic that dictates the proper structure, and management is related to the nature of the critical information flows in that organization. Thus, form is related to function.

The nature of the management of an organization depends on the nature of the critical information required. Internal information flows are those that are used by the organization to perform its functions. Much of this text will be directed toward helping the reader understand how to determine the critical information flows of an organization. If the critical information flows are relatively certain and stable over time, the organization is likely to be characterized by a high level of routineness in structure and management. However, if the critical information flows are relatively uncertain and unstable over time, the organization is likely to have a large number of nonroutine functions creating variability in both structure and management.

Thus, we will describe organization structure in terms of information, information flows, and information processing. Structure consists of the initiation and direction of information flows, standard information flows, task distributions, and the interactions between the information processors in an organization.

Most production operations have predictable and routine information demands. In most research organizations the demands are quite unpredictable; critical information flows have a high degree of variability and operations tend to be nonroutine. While research organizations do have structure, they are in many ways much less rigid than production operations. Lines of command tend to be less clear, task assignments less specific, and work processes less controlled.

A variable that differentiates these two kinds of organizations is the nature of the critical information. What constitutes critical information in most mass-production, assembly-line organizations is very different from what constitutes it in most research organizations. An understanding of the structure and management of the different kinds of organizations requires an understanding of the nature of the information flows.

Because information is a dynamic concept, organizations must be analyzed using a perspective that develops an understanding of the dynamics of a situation. The systems perspective provides such a mechanism.[2] Systems analysis permits the examination of separate elements or subsystems, but it also helps in understanding the relationships between elements.

A mass-production assembly plant will often have several major subsystems. Typically these might be purchasing, production planning and control, plant engineering, personnel, industrial engineering, quality control, and accounting. Each of these subsystems is an organization in and of itself. Yet the structure and management of the total assembly plant cannot be understood by looking at each separately. The total system must be examined, and interrelationships between subsystems must be analyzed. Ignoring any element or set of relationships will lead to a distorted picture. Systems analysis assists in achieving a total perspective of organizations and their critical information flows.

Information Systems Perspective

We have selected an information systems perspective because it is a powerful and helpful way to describe organizations. It provides a useful framework for the student of organizations, the designer of an organization, and the manager of an organization. It should also help each of us who are involved with and interact with organizations during much of our waking lives.

It is useful here to describe an organization briefly using an information systems perspective to aid our understanding. We will consider a typical fast-food restaurant, which Americans often visit. We will select a hamburger restaurant but could have easily selected restaurants serving fried chicken, pizza, or Mexican food. Almost every community has several hamburger restaurants. Over the past twenty years there has been a dramatic change in their operation with the rapid growth of national and regional franchises and chains. While the chains have become more noticeable, most communities also have a number of independents. The independents have only one or at most a few units and are usually owned and operated by local business people.

We need to look at the reasons for the change from local independents to restaurant chains over the past twenty years. Comparing the performance of these two types of hamburger restaurants is quite revealing. The hamburger chains have shown a far greater sales volume per store, and the profit from each dollar of sales and each dollar invested has been higher. Put in the blunt terms of bankruptcy rates, independent hamburger restaurants have failed at a rate that is more than ten times greater than that of hamburger restaurants affiliated with a major chain. Thus, the average investor, owner, or manager is financially better off when involved with a chain-affiliated unit.

Students of organizations, managers, investors, employees, and organization designers are all interested in being able to identify why the major chain units have been so much more successful than the independents. The answer can be obtained by analyzing the manner in which the two different types of hamburger restaurants describe themselves. The major national chains describe themselves in information systems concepts. They pay greater attention to information about factors outside their restaurant (such as eating patterns, customer preferences, and food cost trends) and information on how the functions in their restaurant are performed (such as cooking procedures, greeting customers, determining how much of each food item to order, and determining staffing schedules).

The owner-manager of the independent hamburger restaurant undoubtedly has a lot of information about the operation of the restaurant and its interface with suppliers and customers. But this information is generally not written down. From patterns of success and failure, it is clear that the information held by some owner-managers has led to effective restaurant performance, but for most the lack of written information has led to failure.

The major chains have detailed written documents that cover every operation of the hamburger restaurant: the french fry system, the hamburger grilling system, the cleanup system, and the inventory control system. These documents specify what information the manager and employees should pay attention to. Even the site selection task is standardized by company documents that specify what data must be gathered (such as the population within two miles, the average family size, the average family income, and traffic flows) and then give procedures for analyzing that data (including formulas that calculate sales and profit potential). These documents describe the design of all aspects of the organization; they serve as training tools for the manager and employees; and they give guidelines to be followed in performing daily tasks.

The internal documentation of the hamburger chain organization uses an information systems perspective to describe itself, a description that an increasing number of organizations today are using. For the owner it has meant more profits; for the manager it has facilitated knowing what to do; for the customer it has meant obtaining consistent hamburger quality, service, price, and cleanliness; for the employee it has meant increased understanding of job requirements and expectations.

Organizations and Management

The various elements of an organization do not fit together according to some chance arrangement. Rather, the organization must be managed. There must be a purposeful effort to move the organization toward some desired result. Managers, regardless of their theoretical perspective, seem to attend to the information flows around them.[3] A major purpose of this book is to assist managers by improving their understanding of organizations and the critical information flows that determine organizational functioning.

Management is the process or activity of accomplishing a desired result through the intelligent, rational use of organizational resources. Management is more than getting work done through other people or making a profit for the company. It is a complex set of processes and activities that accomplish the desired results and objectives. The information systems view of organizations can enable managers to accomplish these objectives more effectively and efficiently.

The plant manager of a mass-production, assembly-line organization is concerned about the management of each of the functions in the organization. However, there is no need for the manager to be aware of every detail of each operation. There is a need for the manager to understand the interrelationships among the subsystems and the impact of information flow on the system. When a purchase order is received for a thousand finished products, the manager must coordinate all of the information required to fill that order. If the organization is viewed as a system with interrelated subsystems, then the manager is able to utilize organizational resources better to achieve the desired result.

Organizations Defined

An *organization* is a complex social unit deliberately designed to achieve a specific purpose or set of purposes. One of the classic conceptualizations of organizations is that framed by Cyert and March in their landmark book *A Behavioral Theory of the Firm*.[4] They picture an organization as a coalition of individuals, some of whom are organized into subcoalitions. The *coalition* is defined as a group of individuals that agree to participate in the organization or suborganization. Each coalition has goals that result from a continuous bargaining-learning process.[5] Coalitions are complex social units, and the bargaining process represents a concept of deliberate design. By *bargaining* we refer to verbal and nonverbal interactions between the coalition members to specify and change the organization's objectives. The outcome of the bargaining within a particular coalition is a purpose or set of purposes that gives the organization momentum, direction, and identity.

Characteristics of Organizations

Any organization has distinguishing characteristics. First, there is usually a *locus of power*. The locus may shift frequently or the power may be widely diffused. In a given situation, however, one can identify some point or series of points toward which the power tends to move. This is the locus of power. When the power in a group is so widely diffused as to be unlocatable, or if it shifts so capriciously as to be completely unpredictable, then an organization probably does not exist. "Large organizations are collections of centers of power (and authority), in which the degree of centralization of power varies considerably; that is, in which the relations among the centers of power can vary from highly integrated to highly diffuse."[6] One of the first characteristics to look for in attempting to define an organization is a locus of power.

The second characteristic of an organization is *substitutability of personnel.* In general, organizations are ongoing despite changes in membership. Although a change in membership, particularly a change at or near the locus of power, can cause a significant shift in the nature or character of an organization, the organization will continue to function. Someone else can replace the person who has left without destroying the unity of the organization. This characteristic leads many people to consider organizations as collections of roles rather than of people; they analyze the *role relationships* rather than the people relationships when studying organizations.[7] A *role*, as we use the term, refers to a function or functions that people perform. Therefore, when we look at a restaurant organization we find the roles of chef, waitress, busboy, dishwasher, and cashier. Certainly many of the characteristics of a given role can be influenced by the role occupant, but "roles in organizations, as contrasted with many of the other roles that individuals fill, tend to be highly elaborated, relatively stable, and defined to a considerable extent in explicit and even written terms."[8] It is this concept of *well-defined* roles that allows substitutability of personnel in organizations.

Organizations have a *division of labor among personnel.* This is the third fundamental characteristic of organizations, which can be partly attributed to the differences among roles. Thus, accountants perform one task in an organization and plant engineers perform another. An organization's labor is divided along functional lines according to the roles people assume. Labor may also be divided in ways not related to roles. For example, labor may be divided geographically, as insurance sales forces are, or it may be divided quantitatively, as in the case of multiple assembly lines. In all cases the organization divides its tasks among its members in order to accomplish its goals effectively and efficiently.

The fourth characteristic of an organization is a *history or memory of its past.* Organizations usually capture much of this history in the rules and programs that they use to accomplish their tasks. These are often referred to as the *standard operating procedures.* Through these procedures, the organization remembers its past decisions, sets the pattern for present activities, and anticipates future events.

In general, the procedures most likely to be treated as fixed are those incorporated into the explicit standard operating procedures of the firm. These procedures change slowly and give stability to the organization and direction to the activities that recur constantly. Also, the standard operating procedures influence (and in many cases dictate) the decisions made in the organization.[9]

Not all of the organizational history, however, is incorporated into the standard operating procedures. Much of it is embodied in the traditions, image, and flavor of the organization. Avon is associated with ringing door-bells and Avis with "We try harder." In both cases the history of the organization is caught up in the public image that the organization attempts to project.

Thus, all organizations tend to be characterized by these four factors: a locus of power, substitutability of personnel, division of labor, and a history. In this book, when we speak of organizations, we will be talking about those aggregates of people that exhibit these characteristics. It may help to look briefly at some collections of people that do *not* have these characteristics, which will be called nonorganizations.

Nonorganizations

A mob of people that has gathered in response to a specific, short-term stimulus is a *nonorganization*. It generally has neither a history nor any systematic division of labor. It may be managed and it may have a leader, and it certainly can be studied in an analytical fashion. Mobs do things; that is, they accomplish certain ends that probably would not have been accomplished otherwise. One such end might be to influence the subsequent behavior of a state legislature. Another, though perhaps unintended, end is to cause an unusual concentration of law enforcement officers. But in the sense that the word *organization* is used in this book, a mob is not an organization.

Another example of a nonorganization is a friendship group. Generally speaking, friendship groups do not meet the requirement of substitutability of personnel. A member is chosen because of personal characteristics rather than because of some particular *role* that the individual might assume within the group. Therefore, when one member leaves the group, the replacement is not based on a set of role requirements but is chosen on the basis of the new individual's personal character.

A third example of a nonorganization is what might be called a "situational aggregate." Groups of people such as shoppers, concert goers, or people waiting for a bus are situational aggregates. They seem to behave as a unified whole, and they can be managed (for example, the custom of queuing at a bus stop according to time of arrival serves to manage the people waiting for the bus). Yet these aggregates are not organizations because there is no locus of power *within the group*. Each person is free to act on his or her own and may, for example, enter and leave the aggregate at will. Such situational aggregates are not organizations.

Note that nonorganizations can be studied and managed, and are important both to those who participate in them and to those who do not.

There is a large body of literature on mass psychology, the nature of friendship groups, and the behavior of people in situational aggregates. The concern here, however, is with those social units that have the characteristics associated with organizations.

Because of the rather special characteristics of organizations, management in the organizational setting is particularly important and involves a particular set of constraints. Managers are very much concerned with the locus of power as they influence the distribution and use of organizational resources. A major part of the manager's job may be to define the role relationships within the organization and to provide a mechanism that permits substitutability of personnel. Many managers devote considerable energy to the distribution of work among the organizational members, thus providing for and attending to the division of labor. Standard operating procedures and other evidence of the history of the organization are often maintained by managers; this history, in turn, constrains managers' activities. Organizations, by their very nature, shape the management function.

Organizational Goals

Organizational goals are one of the most important determinants of organizational functioning. We earlier defined an organization as a complex social unit deliberately designed to achieve a specific purpose or set of purposes and the manager's activity as directed toward goal accomplishment. To learn about the nature of an organization and its critical information flows requires an understanding of the processes for forming organizational goals, of the different kinds of goals, of the constraints on goal setting, of the strategies for identifying organizational goals, and of the typical problems that organizations have with goals.

Organizational goals are not fixed in time but are developed through a continuous bargaining process. This process involves a number of interest groups both inside and outside of the organization. Cyert and March view the organization as a coalition of individuals, some of them organized into subcoalitions.[10] In a typical business organization these coalition members might include managers, employers, stockholders, members of the board of directors, regulatory agencies, suppliers, and customers. Over a short period of time specific coalition members can often be identified. Over a long period of time it might be possible to identify only major classes of coalition members. Coalition goals are determined through three major processes:[11]

1. the bargaining process, by which the composition and general terms of the coalition are fixed

2. the internal organizational process, by which objectives are stabilized and elaborated

3. the process of adjustment to experience, by which coalition agreements are altered in response to environmental change

The best goal-setting processes only result in agreement on rather vague objectives. Invariably there are disagreements and uncertainties about subgoals, so that organizations are often pursuing several goals at the same time. Since the existence of unresolved conflict is a conspicuous feature of organizations, it is exceedingly difficult to construct a useful positive theory of organizational decision making by insisting on internal goal consistency. As a result, recent theories of organizational objectives describe goals as the result of a continuous bargaining-learning process.[12]

Goal-setting processes in organizations are dynamic rather than fixed, and the goals are the product of both internal and external forces. Organizations respond to variable information flows and dynamic interactions among subsystems by changing goals as well as by internal accommodation to stresses created by multiple goals. The outcome of coalition bargaining is a set of purposes that gives the organization momentum, direction, and identity.

Categories of Organizational Goals

Organizations have more than one type of goal. Perrow distinguishes five categories of goals.[13]

1. *Societal goals:* relating to society in general. Examples: to produce goods and services, to maintain order, to generate and maintain cultural values. This category deals with large classes of organizations that fulfill societal needs.

2. *Output goals:* relating to the public in contact with the organization. Examples: consumer goods, business services, health care, education. This category deals with types of output defined in terms of consumer functions.

3. *System goals:* relating to the state or manner of functioning of the organization independently of the goods or services it produces or of its derived goals. Examples: the emphasis on growth, stability, profits, or modes of functioning, such as being tightly or loosely controlled or structured. Organizations have options in these areas; the way the system functions and what it generates irrespective of products can become goals for the members.

4. *Product goals* (or *product characteristic goals*): relating to the characteristics of the goods or services produced. Examples: an emphasis on quality or quantity, variety, styling, availability, uniqueness, or innovativeness of the products. Organizations vary widely and deliberately in this respect.

5. *Derived goals:* relating to the uses to which the organization employs its influence in pursuit of other goals. Examples: political aims, community services, employee development, investment and plant location

policies that affect the state of the economy and the future of affected communities. Organizations generate considerable power, which they can use in consistent ways to influence their members and their environments. This power is used independently of product goals or system goals.

When thinking about organizational goals, it is important to clearly specify the type of goal under consideration. Organizations often focus on output goals, yet other goals are important to systems structure and organizational management. For example, if there is a heavy emphasis on the quality of the finished product from a production organization, then quality control and inspection operations will have a commensurate level of importance. If the emphasis is on advanced technology, then the design engineering function will become more important. Emphasis on profits through financial management will lead to the accounting functions assuming a more important role.

Environmental Influences on Organizational Goals

Organizational goals are not independent of organizational setting. Organizations that call themselves "churches" may have difficulty maintaining legitimacy if they become too heavily involved in real estate. Members of a college community see themselves engaged in education and will often call into question a perceived overemphasis on other activities, such as football. A production plant is supposed to produce goods and not protect the environment; therefore, environmental protection activities are often viewed as intrusions on the goal system of the plant. Not only do people within the organization have goal expectations, but those outside may impose limitations on organizational activity based on their perception of the organization. Examples of external forces shaping organizations can be found in the activities of the Environmental Protection Agency (EPA) and the Occupational Safety and Health Administration (OSHA). As a result of congressional mandates, these agencies have imposed a significant set of restrictions on many organizations and have been able to dictate organizational behavior. For most organizations, EPA and OSHA have become very powerful members of the coalition that bargains over societal goals.

Because of the complex bargaining process, the different types of goals, and the external forces that affect goal setting, it is often difficult to determine the real goals of an organization. Advertising will attempt to convince the public that an organization is concerned with a quality product when, on closer examination, it will be discovered that product quality is not a significant goal. There are specific information flows that help us identify the real goals of an organization.

1. *Allocation of resources:* What trends may be discerned from analyses of financial statements of different time periods?
2. *Background of top management:* Whose office is next to the president's? Who is the president today: a lawyer, engineer, or management specialist?
3. *Criteria for promotion:* Does a university reward its professors exclusively for their research and publication or only on their teaching performance?
4. *Customers and suppliers:* Who buys the product or service? Who provides the means for the organization to produce the product or service?
5. *Personal experience of people in the organization:* What kinds of reinforcements or punishments do they receive?
6. *Exparticipants:* Why did they leave? What are their impressions of the organization?
7. *Formal documents:* What are the public purposes as expressed in the articles of incorporation, minutes of board meetings, testimony before official groups, and other public records?

An examination of these information flows will determine the purposes that affect the structure and management of an organization.

Goal Problems

In the process of organizational functioning there are many potential problems with goal systems. These problems can lead to disfunctions in the organization and to inconsistencies in the utilization of resources:

1. The conflict of effectiveness versus efficiency has generated internal problems in many organizations. *Effectiveness* is defined as the degree to which goals are achieved; *efficiency* is an output-input ratio. What relative input level is needed to achieve the goal?
2. Goals that are easy to measure may gain an artificial importance relative to what the organization really wants or needs.
3. Displacement may take either of two forms:
   a. Means-ends reversal: Means displace ends as the goal.
   b. Fixation on internal problems that are not true systems goals: For example, management concentrates on the full utilization of computer facilities without first determining the information needs of the different functional departments.
4. Expansion: A single goal expands and eventually excludes others.
5. Multiplication: An organization tries to do too many different things.
6. Succession: Goals are achieved and the organization must find new things to do.

An organization must guard against these problems if it is to survive. For example, when a local political party gets its candidate elected, it must adopt new goals, such as getting legislation passed, if it is to survive (succession). Or, when an organization preserves the status quo (fixation on internal problems), it may be unable to adopt new technologies rapidly enough to meet the competition. An emphasis on the number of contact hours taught by a university professor (an easily measured goal) may obscure the professor's quality of teaching; or the goal of long-term growth may be so pervasive that an organization is unable to do those things necessary to survive in the near future (means-ends reversal).

Organizations that have good goals are less likely to have problems with their goal systems. Good goals are clear rather than fuzzy, operational rather than unworkable, quantifiable rather than unmeasurable, and challenging rather than unrealistic. Such goals help to clarify structure and management and provide a benchmark against which performance of the system can be judged. One of the purposes of such management strategies as "management by objectives" is to help organizations develop better goal systems. Most performance appraisal techniques for evaluating management effectiveness are enhanced by good goals. Organizations with poor goals tend to flounder, use excessive resources, have many internal problems, and in general be out of control.

Successful organizational analysis requires that careful attention be paid to the goals of the organization. The development of goals must be seen as dynamic rather than static—the result of a continuous bargaining-learning process. Attention must be given to the various kinds of goals present. Constraints on goal setting must be acknowledged, and the environmental press on the goal system understood. The term *environmental press* refers to the pressure that outside individuals and organizations can exert. These outside entities include customers, suppliers, social activists, special interest groups, governmental units, and unions. These members of an organization's environment directly influence its goals. For example, social activists in a community have a very direct impact on the teaching objective (goal) of the local school district. The environment of the nonunion manufacturing firm includes union organizations that influence goals relating to working conditions and wage rates. Care must be taken to recognize the typical problems that organizations have with goals and the characteristics of good goals. Goals are a major determinant of the structure and management of organizations, and understanding goals is a requisite to understanding organizations.

Information Defined

It has been indicated that an important variable in organizational analysis is information. Critical information flows are those that have a significant effect on the structure and management of organizations. Systems analysis is the basic strategy for viewing critical information flows and their impact on subsystems and the relationships between subsystems. At best, information is an elusive concept—an abstraction that tends to lack precision. The following definition will at least tell the reader how the term is used in this book: *Information* consists of meaningful bits of data being transmitted. *Bits of data* are symbols, objects, or physical phenomena (such as light and sound) that have the potential for making an impression on the environment. There are, of course, symbols, objects, and physical phenomena that have no such potential, either because of their state or because of the environment. *Meaningful* bits of data are those that have the potential for influencing a future state of affairs, such as the behavior of a worker, the ease with which a task is accomplished, or the nature of an organizational output. Meaningful bits of data *being transmitted* are flowing from one point to another in a purposeful, orderly manner rather than in a random manner. Information, in other words, consists of symbols, objects, or physical phenomena that have the potential for influencing a future state of affairs and that are flowing from one point to another in an orderly fashion.

Alexander makes the following comment on the definition of information:[14]

The term *information* implicitly assumes existence of usefulness (utility) as distinguished from data (facts) that do not necessarily have any apparent utility. Further, information utility may be realized only when information is transmitted from one data-processing or information-generating system to another. Information when transmitted assumes an economic value because it can modify the behavior of the second system.

It should be noted that information and communication are different concepts. Communication occurs when meaningful bits of data are transmitted (information) by a sender and are recognized and interpreted by a receiver. The thoughts of a company salesman on how to sell to large potential customers written on a memo pad represent information. So does the computer printout of the inventory of parts on hand. Communication occurs when the sales manager reads the memo and the inventory clerk reviews the computer printout. In our analysis we will focus on information and information flows, recognizing that many communications can occur. Because the term *communications* has acquired a very positive connotation in the popular literature, we will not use the term extensively in this book.

The environmental context for an information flow is important because what may be information in one situation may not be in another. Data concerning the cost of steel will be information of great significance for an organization producing automobile engines but may have little or no significance for an organization producing automobile seat covers. While both systems may be aware of the data, only for the engine manufacturer does the data have potential for influencing the future state of affairs. Data about steel costs are extremely significant *information* for this organization, while for the organization making seat covers the same data are *noise*. The seat cover manufacturer is interested in data about the cost of fabrics—not the cost of steel.

Some of the information flowing through an organization is routine and some of it is nonroutine. The impact of each type is different, and it is important to be able to classify a particular information flow correctly in order to analyze the organization's reaction.

Routine Information

Routine information is repetitive, changes very slowly over time, fits into a clearly recognizable pattern, and is easily understood. An organization does not engage in complex search behaviors in order to identify appropriate ways of processing routine information. Because routine information is easily understood, repetitive, and patterned, the system can develop a set of standard operating procedures for processing it.

A mass-production assembly plant regularly receives orders for limited quantities of a given product. These orders are placed by a well-established group of customers with whom the organization regularly does business. There are clearly defined specifications for the product, and each customer orders against these specifications. All orders are placed through customer representatives, who use standard order forms and channel all requests through the production planning and control group. The system has little difficulty in responding to customer requests or in meeting demands in a timely and orderly manner.

The information flows in the above example are routine. A set of standard operating procedures has been developed for processing the information flow. While there may be minor variations, the system can handle these with very limited adjustments and return to normal operations with almost no concern.

Nonroutine Information

Let us suppose that a new customer enters the scene. This customer wants to place a very large order. There is a request for a slight technical modification in the specifications of the product, but the customer is willing to pay a premium price if such a price can be justified by the producer. Because of the size and special nature of the request, the customer wants to deal directly with the plant manager rather than through a customer representative or production planning and control. While there is not an undue rush on the delivery date, the customer wants a quick decision on the organization's ability and willingness to fill the order.

The information flow in this example is nonroutine for this organization. *Nonroutine information* is characterized by a lack of a pattern, a high degree of uncertainty, and a low level of familiarity. Because of this, nonroutine information is difficult for the organization to understand. Nonroutine information cannot be easily classified by the receiver. Involved searches may be required before the complete meaning is understood. In fact, one of the major difficulties that organizations have with nonroutine information is that they may treat the flow as routine or as noninformation in order to avoid complex search procedures. Although the customer wants to deal with the plant manager because of the special (nonroutine) nature of the request, the plant manager may respond by referring the customer to the standard procedures. However, standard procedures appropriate for routine information flows are seldom appropriate for nonroutine information.

Nonroutine information can be classified further as either *continuous* or *discontinuous*. Nonroutine continuous information is marked by comparatively uninterrupted flows. An example is the criteria employed for merit ratings of employees. Rating of employees is a continuous process; however, the criteria used by evaluators are generally not well specified and tend to vary from case to case. The criteria are not really well understood and can seldom be subjected to critical analysis.

Nonroutine discontinuous information is characterized by irregular bursts of information. A sudden rash of employee or customer complaints would be considered nonroutine discontinuous information. The unusual purchase order described in the example given earlier may be nonroutine continuous to the sales manager and nonroutine discontinuous information to the plant manager.

Because of the high cost of search behavior associated with nonroutine information, most organizations tend to treat all information as routine. Nonroutine information is only recognized if the impact on the system is so great that it causes major dislocations. The plant manager will treat the new purchase order as routine until it is recognized as different enough to demand special attention. At that point the system will begin to make serious accommodations for the information flow. A special project manager may be appointed; a schedule review process may be started; new pricing policies may be developed. The system will begin to respond to the nonroutine nature of the information flow.

Routine Information
That Can Be Nonroutine

One key to understanding routine and nonroutine information is to recognize that what may be routine to one system may be nonroutine to another. Therefore, it is necessary to understand the organization and its environment in order to know whether a given information flow is routine. It is not adequate to look at the information flow alone; the system must be understood also. A key difference between two systems is often the information that is considered routine.

The emergency room of a hospital usually considers the medical treatment of accident victims as routine; there is a standard operating procedure for dealing with medical trauma. But the emergency room is poorly equipped to provide care for equally serious but less traumatic illness, such as cancer or tuberculosis. Any analysis of the effectiveness of a hospital emergency room as a complex organization must take into account the limited kinds of medical information that the system considers routine and not expect that the system will be prepared to handle *all* medical information in a routine fashion.

Successful comprehension of the nature of systems information flows is required for the analysis of organizations. The structure and management of organizations vary as the nature of the information flow varies. In later chapters the significance of the information flows on organizational behavior will become more apparent. As activities such as problem solving and decision making are explored, it will become clear how an understanding of these processes depends on an understanding of information flows.

Summary

Organizations are pervasive influences in our lives. Every person is affected by the quality of organizational activity and thus will benefit from a deeper understanding of how organizations work. A key variable to such understanding is information. The information systems perspective is a powerful tool for the analysis of structure and management in organizations. This chapter provides an overview of organizations and information as a basis for further discussion.

The following two chapters discuss information processors and their selective and distortion characteristics. Chapters Four and Five describe organizations as open systems. Chapters Six, Seven, Eight, and Nine cover systems complexity, operations and problem management, and organizational evolution. Chapter Ten is a summary of the use of the critical concepts of the book. Together the ten chapters present an information perspective of organizational theory.

Notes

[1] Alvin Toffler, *Future Shock* (New York: Random House, 1970), chap. 7.

[2] David I. Cleland and William R. King, *Management: A Systems Approach* (New York: McGraw-Hill, 1972), p. 142.

[3] Henry Mintzberg, *The Nature of Managerial Work* (New York: Harper & Row, 1973), p. 29.

[4] Richard M. Cyert and James G. March, *A Behavioral Theory of the Firm* (Englewood Cliffs, N.J.: Prentice-Hall, 1963).

[5] Ibid., pp. 27–28.

[6] Paul E. Mott, *The Characteristics of Effective Organizations* (New York: Harper & Row, 1972), p. 13.

[7] James G. March and Herbert A. Simon, *Organizations* (New York: Wiley, 1958), p. 4.

[8] Ibid., p. 4.

[9] Cyert and March, *A Behavioral Theory of the Firm*, p. 103.

[10] Ibid.

[11] Ibid., p. 29.

[12] Ibid., p. 28.

[13] Charles B. Perrow, *Organizational Analysis: A Sociological View* (Belmont, Calif.: Brooks/Cole, 1970), pp. 135–136. Used by permission.

[14] M. J. Alexander, *Information Systems Analysis* (Chicago: Science Research Associates, 1974), pp. 85–86.

Information Processors

2

Introduction

Information in an organization does not vary randomly but is purposefully manipulated to increase the probability that organizational or individual goals will be achieved. These manipulations are accomplished through the use of information processors.

An *information processor* is any device, technology, body of knowledge, person, or combination thereof that has the capacity to manipulate information in such a way that it is recognizably different after the manipulation. An information processor receives information (input) from its environment, manipulates that information, and transmits its altered information (output) into its environment.

Given the definitions of information in Chapter One and of information processors above, it is easy to see that there are different kinds of information processors. Examples are cameras, production lines, machinery, banks, schools, hospitals, computers, and people. Each of these processes a different kind of information and responds to a specific need.

In addition to the different kinds of information processors, there is great variety within any given set. For example, computers are one kind of information processor, but there are many variations, ranging from simple desk models to sophisticated machines used for highly complex data analysis. Each computer shares certain properties; in particular, each processes information in the form of electrical impulses. But computers differ greatly in their specific characteristics and in the kinds of information that they can process.

The most variable kinds of information processors are people. Airline pilots generally process information that is different from the information that medical doctors process. Engineers and maintenance workers might discuss the same kind of information—how a particular machine works, for example—but they are likely to process it quite differently. Both union leaders and corporate presidents are concerned with the information in a profit-loss statement, but the information will have a different meaning to each, and each will process it quite differently.

An understanding of information processors is required for the analysis of organizational structure and management. Organizations of airline pilots are different from organizations of medical doctors. The role of engineers differs from the role of maintenance men. Organizations that rely heavily on sophisticated computers differ from those that do not. Recognizing the general characteristics of information processors and of the difference between major classes will assist in an examination of organizations.

Characteristics of Information Processors

The first characteristic of information processors is that some are extremely powerful and at the same time extremely limited. The power of an information processor in one dimension is offset by a limited capacity in another dimension. Therefore, organizations have to make trade-offs when choosing an information processor for a given task.

Microscopes can process information about skin tissue, blood cells, imperfections in machine parts, and so on. Telescopes can process information about planets, stars, and the shape and scope of the universe. Both microscopes and telescopes are optical information processors and manipulate light in such a way that the eye (an information processor itself) is able to see things that it would be unable to see otherwise. Both instruments use similar principles of physics, and both are very powerful tools for processing information. Yet they are in no way interchangeable. Despite their power (perhaps because of it) they are both very limited processors of information.

People as information processors tend to have this same characteristic. It has also been observed that highly specialized people are not likely to feel comfortable working in areas outside their specialization. Thus surgeons do not normally practice obstetrics, although both the surgeon and the obstetrician at one time had similar training. People who are highly specialized, who are powerful information processors, predictably have the scope of their information processing skills limited by their specialization.

A second characteristic of information processors is that the more flexible they are, the more complex their internal structure. Flexibility refers to the range of information with which the processor can deal. Managers have to choose between flexibility and simplicity. If one wants a computer that will control a simple machine operation, the computer itself can be simple. If, however, one wants to control an accounting function, then a more sophisticated computer is required. A computer that must manipulate a wide range of organizational variables will be even more complex. The more that flexibility is demanded, the more complexity is needed.

Henry Ford discovered to his dismay that this set of considerations applied to the design of assembly lines. He built a comparatively simple but inflexible assembly line to produce the Model T. The line was extremely effective in processing limited kinds of information in particular kinds of ways, but when circumstances forced more variety into automotive production, Ford found that his information processor lacked the necessary flexibility. He was forced to scrap the assembly line at the cost of millions of dollars. The next one he built had considerably more flexibility and as a result more complexity.

The third characteristic of information processors is that they are specialized. An automobile assembly line is very poor at making watches. Airlines are very inefficient for moving people short distances. A training program for computer programmers does not produce medical doctors. All of these things seem obvious, but they severely limit options in organizations. If an organization has an automobile assembly line but could accomplish its profit goals only by making watches, it has the wrong information processor.

The limitations of the information processor are built into it from its earliest development. Once it is designed, there are constraints on the future kinds of information that can be processed. Although additions can be made to an existing information processor, expansion is limited by the original design. When an initial choice of an information processor or a set of choices for the design of an information processor is made, constraints are placed on future choices.

A fourth characteristic of information processors is that while some flexibility can be built into an information processor, the degree of flexibility is limited. This is because increased flexibility requires sacrificing other characteristics, such as sturdiness and predictability. An adjustable microscope, because of the nature of the microscope as an information processor, can never adjust to become a telescope. A flexible machine tool such as a lathe cannot do repetitive tasks as quickly or as well as a special purpose machine tool. A computer program written to play chess cannot play checkers. Organizations deal with the uncertainty in information flows by utilizing more flexible information processors. This strategy is useful but does not completely solve the problems, because processors have finite flexibility.

Under ideal conditions organizations would like to have information processors that are powerful, flexible, simple, and general in use. While many information processors have some of these characteristics to an extent, none have all at the same time. Part of the continual search for new information processors is created by the need to process new information in new ways.

Conceptual Information Processors

One of the more elusive ideas in this discussion is the notion of conceptual information processors. The ideas that people have are extremely significant manipulators of data in the environment, and conceptual structures might be among the most powerful of information processors, because in many ways they establish the boundaries of information processing. It is important that managers be aware of the conceptual information processors available for use in manipulating information.

Theories   The first class of conceptual information processors is called the *theory*. Theories are sets of assumptions, principles, or rules of procedure devised to analyze, predict, or otherwise explain a set of phenomena. Kaplan defines theory "as the device for interpreting, criticizing, and unifying established laws, modifying them to fit data unanticipated in their information, and guiding the enterprise of discovering new and more powerful generalizations."[1] The quality of a theory is measured by looking at the number of assumptions, the use of previously developed principles, the simplicity of the rules of procedure, and the ability of the theory to help explain a set of phenomena.

An elegant or powerful theory demands a minimum of assumptions—the fewer the better. It uses only a few principles, which have been demonstrated under carefully constructed experimental conditions. The rules of procedure in an elegant theory are clear, simple, and easily replicated under varying conditions. A powerful theory is capable of explaining a wide range of phenomena and can be widely used as the basic building block for a number of subsequent theories. The requirements for an elegant or powerful theory are very stringent, and very few conceptual information processors really meet these tests. There are, however, some well-known theories that fit the criteria. For example, to find the total amount of energy in a given body of matter, all that needs to be known are the mass of the body, the speed of light, and a few simple arithmetic procedures: $E = mc^2$ (where E = energy, m = mass, and c = the speed of light). This comparatively simple theory is, of course, the result of many years of work by Albert Einstein and is the foundation for much of modern physics.

Generally speaking, the theoretical constructs that are useful in organizational analysis do not possess the fundamental elegance of the theory of relativity, but they do provide significant information processing capacity. Keynesian theories of economics help us understand the flow of money in the economy and to control the fluctuations in economic activity through government intervention.[2] Similarly, Vroom's expectancy theory of motivation could be extended to help us understand the effect that controlling information flows to workers has on their willingness to conform to certain patterns of behavior.[3] The liquidity preference theory of interest rate levels provides a psychological explanation for the levels that interest will assume over time and identifies interest as a reward for parting with liquidity.[4] Each of these three theories is a valuable information processor.

The extreme complexity of managerial and organizational behavior makes elegant theory development very difficult. This factor, combined with the difficulty of creating experimental settings for testing, explains the limited number of such conceptual frameworks.

Hypotheses   Another class of conceptual information processors, called the *hypothesis*, is very much in evidence in the managerial world. Hypotheses are assumptions about the nature of things, conjectures that attempt to explain a set of phenomena; they are subject to verification and can be used as a basis for further investigation. A hypothesis usually takes the form "if x, then y." For instance, "If I raise the workers' salaries, then they will produce more units of work per unit time." Or, "If I improve the cash position of the company, then the market price of the stock will go up." Or, "If I increase the computational capacity of the accounting department, then the likelihood of an accounting error will decrease."

It is difficult to prove or disprove these hypothetical statements. The evidence required is difficult to collect and once collected is subject to a variety of interpretations. In addition, there are often a large number of variables that might account for the "then y" statement. Local demonstration of a hypothesis is much more likely than global demonstration, particularly if the limits of the "if x" statements are carefully drawn. "If I raise Joe's salary by 10 percent, then his work output will rise at least 2 percent"—such local demonstrations, particularly when coupled with careful statistical analysis, form the basis of much hypothesis development.

Why are hypotheses valuable if they are at best logical assumptions about possible relationships? In many cases they are the best tools available for understanding the world. But hypotheses are also valuable because they can be tested in a local situation and because once verified they can become useful information processors *over the short run in the local environment*.

Suppose that a man repeatedly discovers that as the cash position of his organization goes up, so does the market value of the stock but with a two-week time lag. He also notices that as the cash position goes down, the stock declines but again with a two-week time lag. Without being able to explain the relationship, he can, if he can control the cash position of the company, manipulate the market value of the stock. (Note: We take no responsibility for anyone who attempts to test this hypothesis.)

Models   The third class of conceptual information is the *model*. A model is a representation of a set of phenomena that is simpler than reality but can be used effectively to help explain or predict reality. The power of a model is not in how close it represents reality but in how much it helps reveal reality. A model must capture the essential elements in a situation without becoming so cluttered with variables that it is impossible to understand.[5]

Organizations are always building models to help them process information flows. One of the most common is the organization chart (see Figure 2-1 for an example of an organization chart for a corporation). An organization chart is a representation of the most observable communication channels and hierarchical relationships in an organization, but many lines of communication exist that are not represented. So the organization chart is understood to be a model of reality, not an accurate and complete picture. Yet the organization chart is a very useful device for understanding some things about an organization.

Figure 2-1. Organization Chart

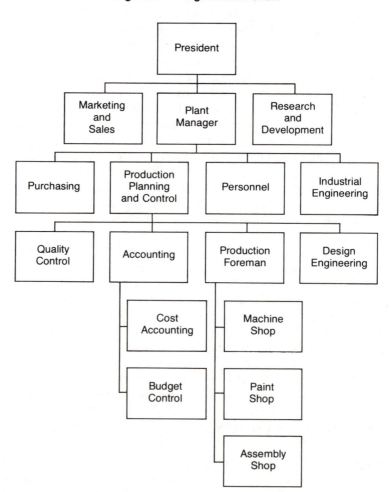

Another model used in organizations is the job description. A typical job description is provided in Figure 2-2. In writing a job description no attempt is made to completely describe everything that the worker does. In fact, any organization whose workers did only those things listed in their job descriptions would soon run aground. People are expected to do many things that are not in their job descriptions, including obvious social things, such as being relatively polite to fellow workers. Nevertheless, the essential elements are included in the job description and these can be used to process many kinds of data. Job descriptions are used to hire workers, train them, and sometimes set their pay scales. In all of these cases the job description is a model to process a flow of information.

Figure 2-2. Typical Job Description

JOB DESCRIPTION	DIVISION: Operations	DATE: 1/20/76
	DEPARTMENT: Industrial Engineering	GRADE: 09

JOB TITLE: Analyst, Work Measurement

SUMMARY

Under guidance of the Supervisor of Methods and Standards or an industrial engineer, conducts work-measurement studies related to all aspects of product manufacturing

1. Develops work-measurement procedures and conducts time-and-motion studies to promote efficient and economical utilization of personnel and facilities
2. Reviews, evaluates, and consolidates standard time summaries
3. Reviews and evaluates work performance and recommends alternate methods for more efficient work accomplishment
4. Analyzes work study data and equipment specifications to establish time and production standards
5. Performs other duties as assigned

EDUCATION AND EXPERIENCE KNOWLEDGE
(ABILITY REQUIREMENT)

1. Normally, must be a high school graduate with two years of specialized training or equivalent in experience.
2. Requires a minimum of one year or related, progressively responsible experience, enabling incumbent to review and evaluate current work procedures and recommend improved and alternate methods

Simplifying Abstractions   Conceptual information processors are the result of the application of abstract reasoning to a concrete problem or situation. Both the strengths and limitations of conceptual information processors are embodied in the fact that they are abstract. Because of this they can be represented symbolically and the symbols can be manipulated in useful patterns without disturbing the environment. Abstractions can be transferred from one person to another, and they permit insights that might be impossible if only the concrete existed.

However, abstractions seldom represent the concrete with absolute accuracy. Therefore, theories, hypotheses, and models can be misleading. The test of the usefulness of conceptual information processors is whether they help the organization to process information.

Technological Information Processors

Technological information processors are those that are available because of technical developments in society over time. These information processors are represented by the hardware of society, and their development has greatly increased the capacity to utilize information in the environment.

Machines   The first class of technological information processors is the *machine*. Simply conceived, machines are devices for using energy to transform information from one state to another. A piece of steel might be transformed into an automobile engine by a very complex metal-working machine, or a piece of leather might be transformed into a belt through the use of a comparatively simple machine. In both cases the hardware of society is being utilized to manipulate bits of data. Some machines make very interesting transformations. A vending machine takes in money and dispenses food directly without any further intervention by the machine operator.

One of the chief characteristics of machines is that they need maintenance. They must be repaired, restocked, oiled, painted, adjusted, and kept in working order. Organizations have developed complex maintenance schedules, but despite these, machines will malfunction at inappropriate times, either refusing to process information or processing it incorrectly.

A second characteristic of machines is that they can only process information within a certain degree of accuracy. No machine can produce a perfectly round ball bearing—every bearing produced is somewhat out of round. Allowances must be made for this deviation from the norm. The less variation that can be tolerated, the higher the cost of the information processor.

A third characteristic of machines is that information processing requires a definable energy input into the machine. Unfortunately, all of this energy input is not translated into information processing, and there is an internal loss within the machine itself. The magnitude of this loss is expressed as the machine efficiency. A machine that is 100 percent efficient could utilize all of the energy input in information processing. Actual machine efficiency is considerably below 100 percent, often around 20 to 30 percent.

The last characteristic of machines as information processors is the general lack of adaptability. Once a machine is designed to process one kind of information in a certain way, it is always difficult and sometimes impossible to get that machine to process functionally different information in significantly different ways. Once one designs a 35-mm camera, there are no attachments to add that will turn the camera into a Polaroid. While many 35-mm cameras are adaptable by using interchangeable lens systems, artificial lights, and different kinds of film, there are are strict limits to the adaptability.

Production Facilities Although many machines are utilized separately as information processors, they can be used in combination. The machine elements may be arranged in a series, for example, when components are transported from one operation to another as shown in Figure 2-3. These elements can also be used in parallel; for example, a number of similar machines may perform the same process in parallel, and then the components are transported to the next operation (see Figure 2-4).

Figure 2-3. Series of Machine Elements in a Production Line

Cutting   Painting   Stapling   Pinning

Figure 2-4. Series of Machine Elements in Parallel

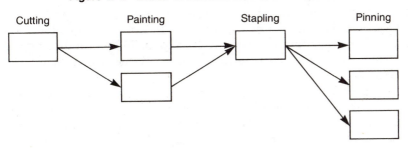

Cutting   Painting   Stapling   Pinning

Organizations are often concerned with the information processing capacity of a combination of machines rather than of any individual machine element. These *production facilities* constitute the second class of technological information processor that must be understood by the manager.

Production facilities, because they are composed of linkages of machine elements, take on all of the characteristics of machines plus other important characteristics. First, the speed of a serially linked group of machines is a function of the slowest element; therefore the total capacity of all except the slowest machine is not usable (see Figure 2-5). The problem can be alleviated by running slower elements in parallel in an effort to equalize the speed of information processing among all segments of the production facility (see Figure 2-6). However, because of limited variability in available elements, it is seldom possible to have all elements operating at full capacity.

Figure 2-5. Time Required by Machine Elements to Perform Their Functions

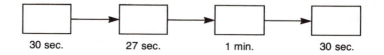

30 sec.   27 sec.   1 min.   30 sec.

Figure 2-6. Use of Parallel Elements to Accelerate Production Rate

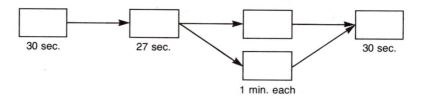

30 sec.   27 sec.   30 sec.

1 min. each

A second characteristic of production facilities is that the probability of failure of the total processor is not the simple sum of the probability of the failure of each individual element. It is necessary to apply the statistics of probability of failure to all information processors—the problem cannot be solved using a simple additive function. For example, a facility produces nuts, bolts, and rods, and one of each item is used in an assembled unit. It has been established that 3 percent of the nuts, 2 percent of the bolts, and 1 percent of the rods turn out defective. The probability of a defective unit, calculated in Figure 2-7, is 0.059 rather than 0.06 (the sum of the individual probabilities).

A third characteristic of production facilities is the critical nature of the links or interfaces between the machine elements. These interfaces must provide for the smooth flow of information from one element of the processor to another. The design of the interfaces is intimately connected to the design of the machine elements themselves. It should also be noted that driving the connecting linkages absorbs energy inputs without contributing directly to the information processing. Thus, interface elements should be as efficient as possible.

Technological information processors are the result of technical and scientific advancements that permit organizations to process new kinds of information in new ways. The major strengths of technological information processors are their power and their predictability. Their major limitations are their limited flexibility and the fact that they are high energy absorbers.

Figure 2-7. Calculation of Probability of Defective Unit

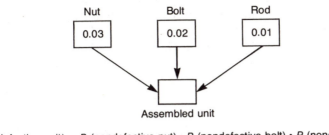

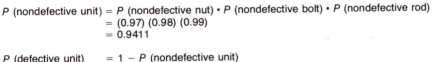

P (nondefective unit) = P (nondefective nut) • P (nondefective bolt) • P (nondefective rod)

= (0.97) (0.98) (0.99)

= 0.9411

P (defective unit)   = 1 − P (nondefective unit)

= 1 − 0.9411

= 0.0589

People as Information Processors

People are critical information processors in most organizations, and meaningful analysis of organizations usually requires an understanding of the ways people function. As we noted earlier, people are also the most variable kinds of information processors and therefore fill a wide range of organizational roles. This flexibility has a price—complexity. Complexity is an organizational problem because it makes people unpredictable and difficult to understand. Why does a worker who has been given explicit instructions sometimes follow them exactly and at other times ignore the most essential step? To what extent does an organizational role shape the worker and to what extent does the worker shape the role? What will be the impact of a given advertising message on the target market? An understanding of organizational structure and management depends in part on an understanding of the factors that influence the behavior of people.

A detailed study of behavior in organizations is beyond the scope of this book. A few elementary observations will, however, contribute to the analysis. If people are seen as important information processing elements in the organization and their strengths and limitations are considered, the nature of the total organization will be clearer.

People process information in two ways. The first is through the use of muscular and structural characteristics of the human body. There are narrow physiological limitations on the ability of unaided human energy to manipulate information. People can only jump so high, lift so much weight, or apply so much force to an object. A primary reason for the development of machines was to overcome human physiological limitations. Technological information processors replace people when the primary task involves the application of energy or force to accomplish a transformation.

Earlier it was shown that one of the major strengths of technological information processors is predictability. This has led some to believe that if people would behave as machines, then organizations would function more effectively and efficiently. Despite considerable investment in such strategies as time and motion studies and work measurement, little progress has been made in making people behave as machines. The natural physiological limitations and extreme complexity of humans have been the major barriers. Instead, it has been more useful to develop technologies that provide power and predictability. This accounts for a rapid development in machines and production facilities that expand the information processing capacity of organizations. In fact, the Industrial Revolution may be viewed as an effort to change the very nature of information processing functions from the use of humans to the use of machines.

It is the second way that people process information that makes them so important to organizational success. This is through the use of the nervous system. The versatility, flexibility, and power of the nervous system are critical considerations when viewing humans as information processors. An important part of the nervous system involves the input functions: the sensory inputs of touch, taste, smell, sound, and sight. Although their range is limited, these input functions are extremely flexible and powerful. The eye is responsive to a wide range of information in the form of light. The ear has the capacity to discriminate among sounds. All of the sensory input mechanisms are extremely versatile. The characteristics of their sensory inputs is a major consideration when trying to understand human information processors. The ability of people to sense environmental changes through their natural input processes is a major determinant of an organization's ability to function.

The vast majority of human information processing is done by the brain in the process called thinking. We define thinking as the organized use of the cognitive structure to process information. The development of cognitive capability is an assimilation of experiences into the existing cognitive structure. Learning represents behavioral changes that result from experience, and it is learning that is responsible for the cognitive development of humans.[6]

As there are physiological limitations on an individual's capacity to produce physical energy, there are similar limitations on cognitive capabilities.[7] Humans can add up a list of numbers only so fast. While people differ in the speed that they can read, there is a limit to the number of lists of information that even the best reader can comprehend per minute. Similarly, there is a limit to the amount of information that humans can keep in their immediate memory. Miller's research indicates that "the span of absolute judgment and the span of immediate memory impose severe limitations on the amount of information that we are able to receive, process, and remember."[8]

Organizations are concerned with people's cognitive structure because this structure determines how information is processed. Organizations will inquire into the nature of an employee's past experiences and training as a clue to present skills and aptitudes. Testing and screening devices are used to ascertain an employee's abilities. Stress interviews and simulated work experiences are used to assess a potential employee's ability to process information under conditions likely to exist in the organization. Through these and other techniques, the organization develops an information processing profile of the potential employee to see if that person will be able to make a significant contribution to organizational functioning.

Because it is seldom true that new employees know everything that is required, organizations are concerned with how cognitive structure develops. An employee is expected to learn how the organization wants its information processed. Many large companies have subsystems that are concerned almost exclusively with training employees; they are responsible for the development of human information processors in much the same way that a factory engineering department is involved in the development of technological information processors.

Groups as Information Processors

Just as production facilities are nonrandom arrangements of machine elements forming a unified information processor, so groups are nonrandom arrangements of people forming a unified information processor. Organizations use groups to increase their information processing capabilities. Increasingly, it is necessary to use groups to achieve objectives, and because of this, some understanding of groups and the group process is required for organizational analysis.

There are two basic criteria for calling a collection of people a group.[9] The first is that there must be a pattern of interaction between the group members. It is not necessary that they conduct interaction face to face or that the interaction be verbal, but it is necessary that the interaction take place. The second basic criterion is that the members be psychologically aware of each other and of the fact that they are members of a group.

Groups exhibit certain characteristics as information processors. Despite changing membership, a group will develop a memory, which will be manifested in the formal record of the group's activities, the precedents for group activity that form over time, and the folklore that surrounds the group. This memory is very useful because it defines the parameters of activity. It is also very useful to organizations as a tool for shaping the information processing capacity of the group. Groups are capable of learning and responding as an entity. Just as organizations are concerned with individual learning, they are also interested in group learning. A group is capable of both emotional and rational reactions to information, and sometimes the emotionality or rationality of a group is a major determinant of how it processes information.

The structure of a group is an important indicator of how information will be processed. Cohesiveness, which is the sum of all of the forces acting on group members to get them to stay in the group,[10] is a central structural property of groups. It is a function of the interpersonal attraction among the members and the number and strength of mutually positive attitudes toward the group and group members. Cohesiveness is increased when members expect that continued membership will lead to important rewards and when other opportunities for members to get these rewards are few. Groups tend to be cohesive when members are similar to each other, when the group faces an outside threat, and when the group has shared success. Cohesive groups tend to have less variation in their information processing than noncohesive groups, to exhibit more aggressiveness, to have a better perception of the task and the situation at hand, and to communicate more with each other. Each of these factors affects the information processing characteristics of the group and therefore affects the manager's ability to use the group as a part of his set of processors.

Groups develop communication networks that affect their ability to process information. Leavitt[11] has studied the performance of five-person groups arranged in four possible networks (similar to the ones shown in Figure 2-8). The circle might represent a group of five salespersons with equal rank and responsibility who are assigned to cover a territory. The chain might represent a situation in a small accounting firm where the chief accountant has two persons reporting to him and each of these has an assistant. The "Y" might represent the structure of an engineering firm with a director of research, an assistant director, a project manager, and two section managers. The wheel might represent the case of a plant manager with four foremen reporting to him.

Figure 2-8. Possible Networks for Five-Member Groups

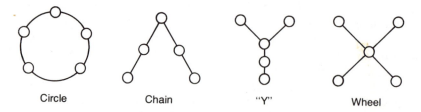

Circle   Chain   "Y"   Wheel

Leavitt's findings indicated that for simple problems with routine information flows, the wheel network was the most efficient and effective, but for complex problems with nonroutine information flows, the circle network was best. In a wheel, when the information is nonroutine and the problem is complex, the central person suffers from information overload and the entire network breaks down. In a circle the work can be distributed more evenly, and there is a tendency for more people to contribute to the problem solution. This shows the importance of the design of the communication network as a determinant of a group's effectiveness as an information processor.[12]

Groups can process information beyond the capabilities of a single individual acting alone, or even beyond the capabilities of a number of individuals acting independently. Within a group the knowledge available for processing new information is greater than the sum total of the knowledge of the individual members, and there is a wider variety of information processing skills. These skills can bring a greater logic to the information processing if there is a norm in the group that permits the members of the group to correct each other.

As with other types of information processors, there are disadvantages to groups as information processors. The social pressure in the group can lead to distortion and make it difficult for the group to function. The goal of the group can shift from information processing to some other goal, such as individual satisfaction. And, of course, using a group for information processing is often expensive. As with other types of information processors, the complexity of groups as information processors leads to flexibility and unpredictability. Organizations are concerned with the trade-offs in using groups as information processors just as they are concerned with trade-offs in using other types of processors.

Organizations as Information Processors

Organizations are, of course, information processors. In general, they are very complex combinations of other information processors arranged in a way that makes it likely that specific, well-defined information transformation goals will be achieved. Information on consumer preferences will be transformed into a marketing strategy by a consumer goods manufacturer. Information on an individual's earnings, assets, and indebtedness will be transformed into a loan limit and interest rate by a financial institution. Death records and causes of death for a given part of the population will be transformed into actuarial tables for setting insurance rates by an insurance firm.

Most organizations are combinations of conceptual, human, and technological information processes. To better understand organizations as information processors and how they differ from the other types of information processors, it is useful to return to our original definition. An information processor is any device, technology, or body of knowledge that may be used to manipulate information in such a way that it is recognizably different after the manipulation. All information processors are similar in that they receive information from the environment and then transmit to their environment the recognizably altered information. Starting in Chapter Four we will discuss systems concepts and the information processors as systems with information inputs and outputs to the environment; organizations represent systems that we are interested in studying. The latter chapters in this text will discuss the organization as a combination of conceptual, technological, and business information processors. Note that the combinations of different information processors represent more than the sum of the individual information processors.

Summary

This chapter has been concerned with defining and elaborating on the five categories of information processors that will be used in describing organizations from an information systems perspective. First, conceptual information processors consist of the theories, hypotheses, and models that provide us with simplifying abstractions to concrete problems and situations. Second, technological information processors represent the hardware of society. These are machines and production facilities that have greatly increased the capacity to utilize information in the environment. Third, people as information processors have tremendous flexibility as a result of our variety of sensory mechanisms and complex cognitive structure. This complexity, which allows people to process more different kinds of information than other information processors, is also a major problem for the organization because it makes behavior difficult to predict. Fourth, groups as information processors consist of a nonrandom arrangement of people that processes information beyond the capabilities of the individuals acting independently. Fifth, organizations as information processors are complex combinations of the other four information processors arranged to accomplish some specific, well-defined information transformation. Understanding organizations requires an understanding of the information processors that comprise them.

Notes

[1] Abraham Kaplan, *The Conduct of Inquiry: Methodology for Behavioral Science* (San Francisco: Chandler, 1964), p. 295.

[2] John Maynard Keynes, *The General Theory of Employment, Interest and Money* (New York: Harcourt, Brace, 1936).

[3] Victor H. Vroom, *Work and Motivation* (New York: Wiley, 1964).

[4] Harry Sauvain, *Investment Management*, 4th ed. (Englewood Cliffs, N.J.: Prentice-Hall, 1973), pp. 92–94.

[5] Russell L. Ackoff, Shiv K. Gupta, and J. Sayer Minas, *Scientific Method: Optimizing Applied Research Decisions* (New York: Wiley, 1962), p. 108.

[6] Roger N. Blakeney, Michael T. Matteson, and Donald R. Domm, "Classical and Instrumental Learning," in *The Individual and the Organization*, ed. Donald R. Domm, Roger N. Blakeney, Michael T. Matteson, and Robert Scofield (New York: Harper & Row, 1973), p. 21.

[7] H. A. Simon, *Administrative Behavior* (New York: Macmillan, 1945).

[8] George A. Miller, "The Magical Number Seven, Plus or Minus Two: Some Limits on Our Capacity for Processing Information," *Psychological Review*, 1956, *63* (2), 95.

[9] Edwin P. Hollander, *Principles and Methods of Social Psychology* (New York: Oxford University Press, 1967), pp. 344–345.

[10] Ibid., p. 362.

[11] H. J. Leavitt, "Some Effects of Certain Communication Patterns on Group Performance," *Journal of Abnormal and Social Psychology*, 1951, *46*, 38–50.

[12] H. Joseph Reitz, *Behavior in Organizations*, (Homewood, Ill.: Irwin, 1977), p. 352.

Information Selection and Distortion

3

Introduction

There are many different kinds of information and many different kinds of information processors. A concern of organizations is to understand the kinds of information that must be processed, how to process the information, and what information processors are available. Given the wide range of alternatives available, an important part of organizational skill lies in making these choices. Obviously the nature of the information that flows within the organization and the transformations that take place must be understood.

All information processors do not process all kinds of information. A camera does not process sound waves, a bank does not process steel, and an airplane pilot does not process medical information. Furthermore, each of these is unique in the kind of information that it can process. A camera does not process all light waves, a bank does not process all financial information, and an airplane pilot does not process all information available about flying. Each selects certain information and acts on that limited set. Organizations are interested not only in the general characteristics of the information processor but also in the way that it selects information; it is through this selection that each processor takes on unique properties.

In addition to selecting information, the information processor also distorts information; it fails to process all of the information that it receives in the intended manner. Another way of saying this is that a certain amount of unplanned information processing takes place. This unplanned information processing, or distortion, causes each individual information processor to be different from every other—even from others of the same general type. Thus, two 35-mm cameras made to the same specifications are not exactly alike because each distorts information differently; although each can select the same light information for processing, distortion takes place. Thus the two cameras, although apparently identical, are different information processors. Two airplane pilots will not process information in the same way either. One who is primarily trained to fly light private planes reacts to phenomena within the environment differently from one trained to fly Boeing 727s. Although both might be called "airplane pilots," each selects and distorts the information about planes and flying in a different manner.

Selectivity of Conceptual Information Processors

Conceptual information processors select a limited set of information related to a given topic and ignore all other information on the topic. For example, the liquidity preference theory[1] of interest rates attends to the psychological information surrounding the setting of interest rates, while the loanable funds theory[2] attends to the information about the market for money. Each attends to information that relates to interest rates, but each selects only a part of the total information available. Since different information is treated by each theory, it is possible to analyze the setting of interest rates using the wrong data with the wrong processor.

Another example of a conceptual information processor that attends to only selected information is the organization chart. An organization chart is a description of the hierarchical relationships and vertical information flows between people or between groups within an organization. It ignores data regarding nonhierarchical relationships and horizontal information flows. The use of the organization chart to discover decision-making or problem-solving processes in the organization can lead to an understanding of vertical relationships within the organization. However, because informal horizontal communications systems within the organization are ignored by the organization chart, the total communications process cannot be understood. Since the informal horizontal communications structure is as important as the vertical in understanding organizational functions, an organization chart must be used with caution—as a conceptual information processor it is limited by its selectivity.

The selectivity of conceptual information processors is determined by the set of assumptions used in developing the processors. When these assumptions are explicit, it is easier to determine strengths and weaknesses of the processor; when they are not explicit, there sometimes are implicit assumptions that limit selectivity. For example, if a particular model of the price-earnings capacity of a company assumes a perfect market and the conditions for a perfect market do not exist, then the model can lead to erroneous policy decisions. Likewise, if a particular marketing policy assumes competition in the marketplace and such competition does not exist, then employing that policy might lead to malfunctions within the company. In both cases, it can be seen that it is necessary to understand the assumptions that determine what information a conceptual information processor will select.

Two apparently similar conceptual information processors may not provide consistent policy considerations. It may then be assumed that one of the conceptual information processors is in error. Sometimes the problem is that the two information processors actually select different sets of information. If the potential for this difference is not apparent and the nature of the information being processed is not examined, then bad judgments about which information processor is needed for a given task will result.

Conceptual information processors are classified in order to help identify the information likely to be selected. One such classification system groups them according to the basic disciplines with which they are associated. We have accounting information processors (capital budgeting techniques), marketing information processors (consumer surveys), management information processors (organization charts), and so on. Such classification schemes, which arrange conceptual information processors by discipline, ignore the interrelatedness of various informational phenomena in the environment. In an effort to overcome this, conceptual information processors are often classified by institutions; thus there are sets of conceptual information processors that relate to banking, insurance companies, small businesses, and production operations.

This jumble of conceptual information processors arranged by discipline as well as by institution is confusing. Even being aware of the large number of conceptual information processes available does not necessarily help to categorize and arrange them in a way that identifies what information each will select from the environment and how each will process that information. There must be a plan to facilitate a choice of the correct conceptual information processor to deal with a given flow of information. The various schemes for classifying information processors (by discipline or institution, for example) will help. Consider the case of a loan officer at a bank. Before lending funds to a firm, the officer may be required (1) to analyze the firm's income statements and balance sheets for the current year, as well as for previous years (accounting information processor); (2) to take into consideration the current prime interest rate (finance information processor); (3) to evaluate the firm's latest consumer surveys (marketing information processor); and (4) to evaluate the competence of the firm's management, for example, management's success in previous decision making (management information processor). Each of these activities requires the use of a variety of conceptual information processors. Choosing the right ones requires knowledge of the selectivity characteristics of a wide variety of possible choices.

Selectivity of
Technological Information Processors

Just as conceptual information processors are selective in terms of the kinds and types of information that they process, so are technological information processors. To the uninitiated, a wood lathe and a steel lathe may look very similar. In fact, both operate according to some of the same principles. However, a wood-turning lathe will not process steel and a steel-turning lathe will not process wood. Each is limited as a technological information processor to the types of information flows that it will accept. The transmission of radio signals over microwave channels is significantly different from transmitting radio signals over standard telephone cables. Even a person's ability to use credit is restricted by the ability of the information processor to select the appropriate information: The person with Master Charge cannot be recognized by a computer system that operates on data utilizing American Express.

Even very similar technological information processors are designed to select only limited data. In the general class of information processors called "automobile," those processors that are designed to run at the Indianapolis 500 cannot process the same kind of gasoline that those designed to run on an interstate highway do. In fact, two automobiles that are both designed for interstate highways might not even use the same kind of gasoline.

Control of the kinds of information that a processor will select from the environment is built into its design from its inception. Once a conceptual information processor model of an organization is formulated to understand the decision-making functions within the organization, the kinds of information that will be selected and processed by that model are already limited. Likewise, once a telephone transmission system is designed, the kind of information to be selected by that technological information processing system is already determined. Even in the preliminary stages, it may be obvious what selectivity features are being incorporated as the processor is being designed.

Distortion of
Conceptual Information Processors

In addition to the fact that each information processor selects from the environment certain information that it will attend to, it is also true that each distorts the information that is processed in a unique way. By *distortion* is meant that there is a certain amount of unplanned information processing that takes place. Managers must be aware of the distortion characteristics of each information processor in order to select an appropriate processor for the tasks to be done. Because it is impossible to have an information processor that does not distort information, managers must be able to tolerate information distortion.

Conceptual information processors distort information by oversimplifying it. Information about an organization's vertical communications system is distorted by the organization chart because the difficulty or ease of transmission in the vertical system is ignored. A supervisor's relationships with five employees may seem to be equal according to the organizational chart, but if it was known that one of the employees was the supervisor's next-door neighbor, then it would be understood that the vertical relationships between the supervisor and the five employees might not be equal. Thus, the organization chart oversimplifies the relationships. A conceptual information processor that describes motivational patterns in a work force tends to oversimplify the ability of the manager to motivate workers. For example, Vroom's expectancy theory of motivation[3] is useful in helping to understand motivational patterns, but it tends to oversimplify the factors that contribute to motivation, and so it distorts the phenomenon.

Sometimes, of course, the conceptual information processor may make an information transformation appear more complicated than it really is. For example, in representing how decisions are made in the organization, the organization chart might imply that it is necessary to go up a hierarchical chain of command when in reality some decisions can be made in other ways.

Distortion of Technological Information Processors

Technological information processors also distort information. A radio amplifier adds information to the radio signal that makes the sound that the listener hears different from the sound that was originally put into the system. We often call this particular kind of distortion "noise" and try to eliminate it. A production plant that is responsible for manufacturing automobiles distorts the information it receives, and each of the automobiles it produces is therefore different, not only from each other but also from the plan specified in the design of the production system. A camera lens does not transmit and process all information perfectly. If a particular lens curvature is designed to achieve a certain magnification and the lens is ground to specifications, there will be a loss of certain light rays within the lens itself as a result of the grounding. In each of these cases the technological information processors fail to process information perfectly.

Organizations realize the inability of information processors to operate according to a perfect plan and build an allowance for deviations into their information processing systems. Cost is one of the factors affecting an organization's willingness to tolerate deviations from plans. Generally speaking, the less distortion in an information processing system, the more costly the system.[4] Therefore, organizations must decide if they are willing to invest the resources required to reduce distortion.

If information must be processed quickly, it is often necessary to tolerate large amounts of distortion. For example, if plant productivity must be estimated quickly, it is likely that a simple conceptual model will be used, thus yielding an estimate with a low degree of accuracy. However, if there is enough time, a more sophisticated conceptual model can be used, perhaps involving such elements as computer simulation, to arrive at a more accurate estimate. The factor of time often affects the amount of distortion that can be permitted within an information processing system.

All information processors are selective and all information processors distort information. The tendency of many students and managers of organizations to ignore these factors can create considerable problems in organizational analysis.

Selectivity of Human Information Processors

Limited Physiological Capacity   People do not react to all available information in their environment. The physical characteristics of human sensory mechanisms determine the capacity of the system to respond. The range of sound waves audible to the human auditory system limits the sound information that can be processed; the range of light waves visible to the human eye limits the visual information that can be processed. Bobbitt and his associates stated, "Indeed, our sense organs are often bombarded with stimuli of which we never become aware. Our eyes, for example, have certain absolute thresholds, and stimuli whose energy levels are below these thresholds are never sensed."[5] In addition to the selectivity forced upon the human information processor by the range limitation of sensory mechanisms, the sense organs tend to be more responsive to some inputs than to others, even if both are within the normal range. For example, if one noise is loud and another soft, the ear tends to select the loud noise. This does not mean that information contained in the loud noise is more important than the soft noise, but it does mean that the information processor is selecting the information to be attended to not on the basis of content but on the basis of magnitude.

The information that the human information processor selects from the environment is a function of the limits of the sensory input mechanisms. The sensory mechanisms of the human information processors provide the interface functions between the environment and the nervous system. The sensory input functions are seeing, hearing, touching, tasting, and smelling. Each responds to a set of information inputs from the environment. These inputs may take several forms, such as sound or light, but each is characterized by a change in energy state in the external environment that is recognized by the sensory mechanism. People sense not only the presence or absence of light, but also differences in intensity and color. It is possible under certain conditions to notice an energy phenomenon with more than one of the sense mechanisms. For example, the rays from the sun are both light to the eyes and warmth to the skin.

There is a minimal level at which a change in information can be noticed with the unaided senses. This minimal level is called the "difference threshold," the "discrimination threshold," or the "just noticeable difference" (usually abbreviated JND).[6] It is important to be aware of the JND in information levels. If a supervisor wants a worker to respond to a change in the sound of the operation of a machine, that change must be above the JND or the change will not be noticed. If it is necessary for a worker to be able to discover visual defects in a manufactured part, then it is necessary that the magnitude of the visual defects be above the JND. One way to overcome the limitations in the ability of the human information processor to discriminate between small changes in information inputs is to magnify those changes, usually through some kind of technological information processor, such as a lens or amplifier. These bring small information inputs that would not be noticeable to the unaided sensory mechanisms into the noticeable range. We need to account for the range of inputs that can be accepted or selected by a given sensory mechanism. Also, within that range, we must attend to the just noticeable differences that enable the human information processor to recognize change.

Sensory mechanisms are not equal in their ability to respond to information inputs. Human information processors are more sensitive to visual information than to any other kind. Approximately 70 percent of the nerve endings in the body are devoted to activities of the eye, a complex and sensitive information processor. By contrast, the sense of taste is an ill-defined and poorly used information processor, as is the sense of smell. Because of the tremendous commitment of human information processors to visual inputs, much of the world is organized in response to visual inputs. While this visual emphasis indicates the kinds of information inputs that are most readily accepted by the human information processor, it also means that selection of visual inputs is important in the total functioning of the human information processor.

Perceptual Readiness   At the same time, some information available to the sensory mechanisms is not processed but is selected out or blocked before any processing takes place. The information selected from the environment is also a function of the person's need state and past experiences. When driving down the highway, one does not see all the gasoline stations or roadside eating places, although they exist and at times can make a strong impression on the sensory mechanisms. A person selects only elements of information in the environment that are relevant; when the car is low on fuel or the driver is hungry, gasoline stations or eating places "appear."

Not only do human information processors select information on the basis of the capacity of the various sensory mechanisms, but they also select information from the environment based on the state of the information processor. The readiness of the human information processor to select information from the environment is called perceptual readiness.[7] Perceptual readiness is the ease with which information is recognized, and it reflects both present needs and past experience. People tend to select information from the environment when they expect the information and when they feel that the information is relevant to their needs.

If a manager wants a worker to select certain information from an environment, the worker must expect it and feel that it is relevant. For example, a person usually seen in a particular setting may not be noticed out of that context. If while at a football game a man needs a doctor and begins to search the faces in the crowd, his need for a doctor will help him to perceive the information that the person four rows away is his family doctor. He had ignored that information previously because he was not expecting the doctor at the football game. So it is the combination of a person's need state and the degree to which he or she expects a bit of information to be in a particular environment that determines perceptual readiness.

In addition to the factors of expectation and need state, the sequence of an information flow affects perceptual readiness. When the sequence is broken or unnatural, it is less likely that information will be perceived. A train whistle suggests a train is coming and increases the perceptual readiness to see the train. Hearing a train whistle will not be surprising to someone standing near a railroad track but will be very surprising to someone driving on an interstate highway.

Situational Characteristics Another factor affecting whether a person processes a particular bit of information is the complexity of the environment itself. The more types of information in a given environment and the more ambiguity that exists in selecting the information, the less likelihood there is that a particular bit of information will be selected. Managers want workers to select the information relevant to the organization from all of the information that exists in the environment. They try to create an environment in which only the relevant information is present. This enables the worker to select and process relevant information more easily.

Another factor that affects the ability of people to select information from the environment is the stress under which they are operating. If a person is required to make judgments without adequate time to attend to all sensory inputs in the environment, then that person is not likely to select truly important information. When people are forced to work under highly stressful conditions, their ability to select information from the environment is reduced and they are prone to miss information that is important. This suggests that when high stress is present, such as under high-speed conditions or under conditions of high anxiety, there is a greater likelihood of erroneous perception or of failure to select the appropriate information from the environment.[8]

Thus, the three main factors affecting the ability of human information processors to select information from the environment are: the capacity of the sensory input mechanisms, characteristics of the need state, and the nature of the situation.

Distortion of
Human Information Processors

After selecting the information to be processed, the human information processor distorts it so that what is seen is not simply objective reality. Perceptions are not copies of the real world but are influenced by a number of factors, including the environment, previous experiences, and the present state of the processor. Distortion characteristics of human information processors are influenced by some of the same factors that influence selectivity capacities—the environment, previous experiences, and the present state of being.

First, a given information input for a human information processor is distorted by the nature of concurrent information inputs from the environment. For example, if a person hears a particular noise at the same time that he or she sees a particular event, the noise will have one meaning. But when it is not heard at the same time as the event, the sound is likely to have another meaning.

Second, distortion is created by the nature of previous experiences. Previous experience with a particular set of information determines how new information is perceived. A person who has been in a bad car accident will interpret the sound of another car accident differently than if that person had not been in a car accident. If the person has just recently bought a certain make of car, that person will be more likely to see other cars of that make on the road than if he or she had not bought that particular model.

Third, the condition of the information processor itself, or the state of a person, determines the degree to which he or she is likely to distort information. If a person is under high stress, that person is more likely to misinterpret information than if he or she is not. If a person is angry, a particular remark made by a friend may seem to take on quite a different meaning than if the person is not angry; thus, the state of the receiver determines how information is distorted. All of these factors interact to determine the way that people as information processors select, distort, and perceive information in their environments.

Clearly, because of the number of factors that are involved in the perceptual mechanisms, no two people perceive information in the same way. There will be physical differences, differences in previous experiences and knowledge, and differences in their present state. Therefore, what appears to one person as one bit of information may appear as another bit to another person. Two people who are observing the same phenomenon are distorting and selecting the information relative to that phenomenon differently. For example, when two people look at a third person, they will perceive different sets of characteristics about that person. An extremely tall or short person is more likely to notice height than a person who is of average height. Sometimes differences in people's perceptions of a situation are critical to the functioning of the organization.

Organizations must be aware of the information processing characteristics of human information processors and the kinds of information that human information processors can select from the environment in order to make effective use of people in meeting goals. Managers must be aware of the nature of the environment in which human information processors are going to operate if the managers want the workers to perceive the important information. For example, it is difficult for people to discriminate between small changes in sound if they have to operate in a noisy environment. In addition to the basic physical nature of the selection mechanisms and the environmental impacts on selection and distortion, managers must be aware of the state of the person at the time the information is being selected and distorted. As a part of their understanding the present state, managers need to be aware of the previous experiences of the person in order to have some idea of what information will most likely be processed. In many cases managers will want to alter their employees' experiences through training to decrease perceptual variances.

Selectivity and Distortion
Characteristics of Groups

Just as individuals have certain factors that influence their selection and distortion of information, so do groups. However, a group's characteristics as an information processor are not simply the sum of the individual characteristics of the members or an algebraic average of the members' characteristics. In some ways groups can select more information from the environment than individuals, but in other ways groups are more limited. The interaction patterns that exist between the members of a group, through which the members are aware of each other psychologically, lead to particular group characteristics. A group is greater than the sum of its parts, but the nature of a group is a function of the relationships among the members and the characteristics of the group as a group.

What are some of the characteristics of a group that affect its ability to select and distort information? One of the major characteristics is a group's goals. Goals limit the information selected because they focus the group's attention on certain bits of information and permit other bits of information to be ignored that might, if attended to, affect the group's behavior.

Another group characteristic that affects selectivity and distortion properties is group cohesiveness. Earlier, cohesiveness was defined as the sum of the forces that attract the members of the group to stay in the group. Group members in cohesive groups tend to assess more accurately the other members as well as the tasks that must be accomplished. Cohesive groups have better systems of internal communications and therefore are more likely to select relevant information from the environment and to distort that information less than noncohesive groups. However, highly cohesive groups will be consistent in their selectivity and distortion patterns, and it will be very difficult to change these patterns.

The communications structure within a group affects its ability to process information. (You will remember that in Chapter Two, we outlined some of the various communications structures that can exist within a group.) Those groups that have communications structures that are appropriate to the tasks will process the information in the environment more accurately and distort it less than those groups that do not have the appropriate communications structure.

Another condition that affects the ability of a group to process information is whether the group is in a competitive or a cooperative arrangement with other groups.[9] Those that are in a highly competitive arrangement tend to focus on the other group's behavior rather than on relevant information and on reducing distortion. Groups that are cooperative both with other groups and internally are more likely to focus on all relevant information, not just the information about the other group, and are less likely to distort information that they receive. The effects of competition on group behavior are similar to the effects of stress on individual behavior.

One of the major factors that influences the way a group selects and distorts information is the group's leadership. Every group has a need for certain leadership acts, including goal focus, interaction facilitation, interpersonal support, and work facilitation.[10] When a group has leadership that provides these elements, it is able to spend less time on internal maintenance and is better able to select relevant information from the environment with minimum distortion.

Thus, the main elements that affect how groups process information are group goals, cohesiveness, competition, and leadership.

Group Influence on Individual Perception

Both groups and individuals have unique characteristics as information processors. One of the effects that belonging to a group has on individual members is on perception. People, because they are group members, perceive things differently than if they were not in the group.

Perhaps the most well-known experiments that have been conducted to illustrate this point are those by Asch.[11] He found that some people were unable to withstand group pressure and that they denied information that under other circumstances would be clear and unambiguous. As the information became more ambiguous, increasing numbers of people conformed to group pressure. There were wide differences between the reactions of people to group pressure, some people being able to withstand it much better than others. Asch also found that the structural properties of the group were important factors in the group's ability to influence a person; a highly cohesive group was more effective in modifying an individual's perception than a slightly cohesive group.

During World War II, Lewin conducted a set of experiments on the effect that groups have on shaping an individual's perception. He asked some persons to commit themselves to a certain position while they were members of a group and others to commit themselves to the same position individually. Those who made the commitment as part of a group were much more likely to behave in accordance with that commitment than were people who were acting as single persons.[12]

What is the meaning of these phenomena to the organization? They are important when an individual is faced with an ambiguous situation in which it is difficult to establish social reality, for example, what constitutes a fair day's pay? When under the influence of a cohesive group, such as a well-organized union, a person's perception of reality—how much money one should earn—is more likely to be influenced by the internal information flows within the group than by other, more objective information flows. Thus, the organization cannot ignore group effects on the behavior of individual information processors.

Summary

This chapter has been concerned with the selectivity and distortion characteristics of information processors. We have considered the degree to which conceptual and technological information processors tend to select and distort information based on certain characteristics of the environment, the information, and the processor. We have also noted certain ways in which people as individuals and people in groups select and distort information. From this we can see that organizations must be aware of the particular characteristics of people as information processors and also recognize the uniqueness of each individual information processor. Because of variance among information processors, there is a need to develop a range of tolerance limits within which information must be accurate. The danger, of course, is that a given information processor may not select the correct information from the environment or that the information may be distorted to such a degree that it causes managers to do the wrong thing and the organization not to achieve its goals.

Notes

[1]Harry Sauvain, *Investment Management*, 4th ed. (Englewood Cliffs, N.J.: Prentice-Hall, 1973).

[2]Harry D. Hutchinson, *Money, Banking, and the United States Economy*, 2nd ed. (New York: Appleton-Century-Crofts, 1971), pp. 264, 268.

[3]Victor H. Vroom, *Work and Motivation* (New York: Wiley, 1964).

[4]Dan Voich, Jr., et al., *Information Systems for Operations and Management* (Cincinnati, Ohio: South-Western, 1975), p. 231.

[5]H. Randolph Bobbitt, Jr., et al., *Organizational Behavior* (Englewood Cliffs, N.J.: Prentice-Hall, 1974), pp. 87–88.

[6]James Drever, *A Dictionary of Psychology*, rev. Harvey Wallerstein (Baltimore, Md.: Penguin, 1964), p. 149.

[7]J. S. Bruner, "Social Psychology and Perception," in *Readings in Social Psychology*, 3rd ed., ed. E. Maccoby et al. (New York: Holt, Rinehart and Winston, 1958), pp. 85–94.

[8]See S. E. Asch, "Effects of Group Pressure upon the Modification and Distortion of Judgements," in *Groups and Organizations: Integrated Readings in the Analysis of Social Behavior*, ed. Bernard L. Hinton and H. Joseph Reitz (Belmont, Calif.: Wadsworth, 1971), pp. 215–222.

[9]Leo Keith Hammond and Morton Goldman, "Competition and Non-Competition and Its Relationship to Individual and Group Productivity," in *Groups and Organizations: Integrated Readings in the Analysis of Social Behavior*, ed. Bernard L. Hinton and H. Joseph Reitz (Belmont, Calif.: Wadsworth, 1971), pp. 339–348.

[10]David G. Bowers and Stanley E. Seashore, "Predicting Organizational Effectiveness with a Four-Factor Theory of Leadership," in *Groups and Organizations: Integrated Readings in the Analysis of Social Behavior*, ed. Bernard L. Hinton and H. Joseph Reitz (Belmont, Calif.: Wadsworth, 1971), p. 179.

[11]Asch, "Effects of Group Pressure," pp. 215–222.

[12]Kurt Lewen, "Group Decision and Social Change," in *Readings in Social Psychology*, ed. T. M. Newcomb and E. L. Hartley (New York: Henry Holt and Co., 1947).

Organizations
as Systems

4

Introduction

Up to this point the primary concern has been with the variety of elements that must be understood if the organization as a whole is to be understood. Information has been highlighted as the key variable in organizational functioning, and the basic characteristics of an information flow have been noted. The concept of information processor has been introduced and various kinds of information processors have been described. General properties of information processors were discussed with particular emphasis on selection and distortion characteristics. It has probably become apparent that organizations are very complex, if for no other reason than that there is a great variety of information and information processors utilized to achieve organizational goals.

Understanding this complex interaction is very difficult but is facilitated with the use of systems thinking to model or describe the organization. The purpose of this chapter is to develop a conceptual framework for thinking about organizations as systems. This conceptual framework will provide a meaningful strategy for understanding the complex interaction of information and information processors and thereby understanding the very nature of organizations.

Systems Defined

In its simplest sense, a *system* is a combination of information processor, information flows, and interactions, and can be diagrammed as in Figure 4-1. For the sake of simplicity, this discussion of systems will assume only one information flow and only one information processor. The reader should be aware that all real systems consist of a number of information flows and a number of information processors. However, the assumption here does no violence to the basic concepts required for understanding real systems.

Figure 4-1. Information Flow

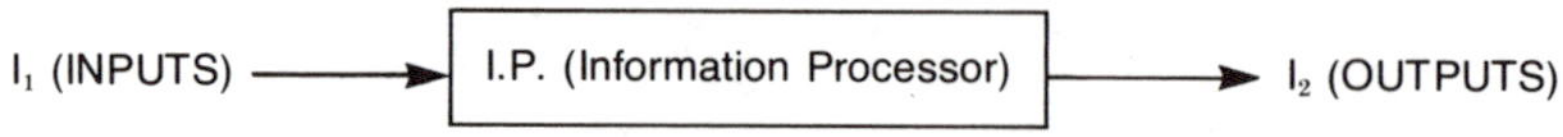

I₁ (INPUTS) ⟶ | I.P. (Information Processor) | ⟶ I₂ (OUTPUTS)

Recall that an information processor has been defined as any device, technology, body of knowledge, person, or combination thereof that has the capacity to manipulate information in such a way that it is recognizably different after the manipulation. Although information inputs (I_1) and information outputs (I_2) are part of the same information flow, $I_1 \rightarrow I_2$, they are not equal; that is, $I_1 \neq I_2$. But they are functionally related, and this relationship can be expressed as follows:

$$f(I_1) = I_2.$$

This equation represents a model of the system shown in Figure 4-1. A description of the properties of the information processor, I.P., is a description of the function, $f()$, and it is the nature of this function that determines the transformation $I_1 \rightarrow I_2$. When it is stated that $f()$ is an identifiable, functional relationship between I_1 and I_2, this suggests that the relationship between the components of the system, $f(I_1) = I_2$, is not random. That is to say, given any two components, the third is defined *if there is a system*. Thus,

1. If I_2 is an automobile and $f()$ is an automobile production line, then if there is a system $f(I_1) = I_2$, the nature of I_1 is not random.
2. If I_2 is an automobile and I_1 is a set of component parts for automobiles, then if there is a system $f(I_1) = I_2$, the nature of $f()$ is not random.
3. If I_1 is a set of component parts and $f()$ is an automobile production line, then if there is a system $f(I_1) = I_2$, the nature of I_2 is not random.

A system is more than just a collection of elements. It is a combination of information flows and information processors that are connected through some interactive relationships such that $f(I_1) = I_2$.

This definition of systems is in agreement with others that have been widely used. One of the best known is that of Russell L. Ackoff: "A system is an organized or complex or unitary whole. It is a set of interrelated elements."[1] De Greene used a definition that is more complex but that captures the purposefulness of systems: "In the most general sense, a system can be thought of as being a number of set constituents or elements in active organized interaction as a bounded entity, such as to achieve a common whole or purpose which transcends that of the constituents in isolation."[2]

Some writers tend to focus attention on the information processor rather than on *both* the processor and the information flow, but both are, of course, equally important. Not only are the elements themselves of concern, but the interaction between them is also a significant part of the systems concept; the dynamic nature of systems, which is fundamental to almost all conceptualizations of systems theory, should be captured in the very definition of a system.

The basic components of a system are traditionally labeled "inputs"—the equivalent of our I_1, "outputs"—the equivalent of our I_2, and "process"—the equivalent of our I.P. Figure 4-1 can be relabeled as follows:

Figure 4-2

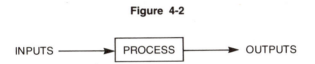

INPUTS ⟶ PROCESS ⟶ OUTPUTS

Figure 4-2 is the simplest model of a system that is normally found in the systems literature, and this model will generally be used as the basis for discussion throughout the remainder of this book. However, the notations I_1, I.P., and I_2 will be used where they are more appropriate or illustrative.

It is not adequate for systems to have elements of input, process, and output alone. All real systems also have feedback and feedforward loops that allow for systems control and planning. *Feedback* has been defined as "that function of the system which automatically brings back information about a situation under consideration to the source of that information."[3] Certain portions of the systems output are returned to the system as input and are used to compare the present state of the system to the desired state; that is, the *actual* outputs are compared to the *desired* outputs or goals to determine if the performance of the system is satisfactory. Information in the feedback loop is used to control a system. Figure 4-3 shows a system with the feedback loop.

Figure 4-3

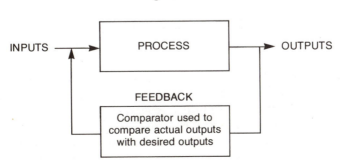

INPUTS ⟶ PROCESS ⟶ OUTPUTS

FEEDBACK

Comparator used to compare actual outputs with desired outputs

While feedback is utilized for control purposes, feedforward loops provide information that is used for planning purposes to develop expectations about the future state of the system.[4] Critical input information is run through a simulator that acts like the processor, and outputs of the simulator are compared with desired outputs or goals of the system. Since the simulator's behavior closely resembles the processor's behavior, the outputs of the simulator can be used for planning the future behavior of the processor. Figure 4-4 shows a system with the feedforward loop. Figure 4-5 shows a system with both feedback and feedforward loops.

Figure 4-4

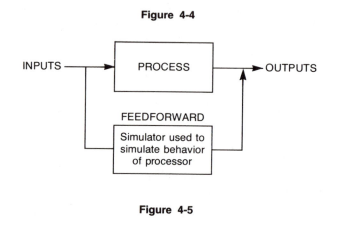

Figure 4-5

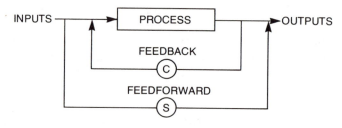

In order to improve understanding of these components of a system, the next sections of this chapter and the following chapter describe the general characteristics of each component.

Inputs

Inputs to a system include all of the information flows that influence the system. As such, systems inputs are a major constraint on systems functioning; as a result, awareness of their general characteristics is required to understand the nature of a system. For example, if a person knew the different kinds of people that were employed by a firm and had a general idea of the number of employees in each job classification, one could begin to develop a real understanding of the nature of the firm. Let us suppose that there are more sales engineers employed by firm A than any other kind of employee, while firm B employs more technical engineers. Because salespeople tend to be heavily involved in interpersonal interaction and technicians do not, it can be hypothesized that firm A will be much more people oriented than firm B. To understand these two firms, it is useful to know the ways in which they differ in employee input characteristics.

Another example of how knowledge of inputs helps in understanding a system can be seen by observing two restaurants. The one that has a small quantity of high-quality food as inputs will generally be quite different from the one that has a large quantity of low-quality food. In fact, the relative price of a meal in these restaurants could be fairly accurately predicted by observing the nature of the inputs.

In both of the above examples, an understanding of the inputs has given significant clues for understanding the systems. Some methodologies for using inputs as a major element in systems analysis are quite sophisticated. In some industries it is possible to estimate very accurately the cost and time of production from a careful analysis of a list of materials that itemizes the inputs for the finished product. These methods of cost and time estimation have been developed as a result of careful determination of the probable impact of a given input information flow on the system.

Known and Unknown Inputs   In every real system, some characteristics of inputs are known and others are unknown (see Figure 4-6). Because of the complexity of information flows, it is virtually impossible to know everything about all inputs. It is even likely that there will be some inputs about which nothing is known, at least until significant effects of the input on systems functioning are detected.

Figure 4-6

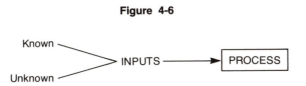

When a worker is hired by an organization, the organization usually collects a good bit of data in an effort to know the worker. Investigations are conducted into educational background, past employment history, health status, and other factors. The extent of the inquiry is a function of how important an input the organization thinks this particular employee will be. If the employee is to work in a nonsensitive job on a production line, then the data collection process might only involve asking the employee to complete a simple one-page application. If, on the other hand, the position being filled is a key executive slot, then the data collection process will likely be extremely complex and time consuming. Not only will the employee be investigated but inquiries about family will also be conducted. Despite careful efforts, there will still be some unknown elements of this input, which can have a significant impact on the system.

In buying steel for a machining process, a person is expected to know a great deal—including such things as tensile strength, purity, hardness, and carbon content—prior to making the purchase. But it is much more likely that someone will purchase water from the city with almost no knowledge of potentially important variables such as purity, hardness, and sulfur content. The amount of knowledge that the organization has about its raw materials varies widely. Because of differences in beliefs about the importance of various informational inputs, there are differences in the degree to which the organization attempts to know about inputs.

In fact, there is likely to be a large number of systems inputs about which almost nothing is known. For example, each employee brings to the work place a wide range of knowledge about a wide range of topics. Except in unusual circumstances, almost no effort is made to assess the variety of skills and talents of employees, even though these proficiencies may be of great value to the organization.

Yet it should not be assumed that organizations are completely oblivious to inputs. A good bit of organizational energy is spent in trying to discover the nature of inputs, moving things from the unknown to the known. Much of the incoming inspection effort of manufacturing plants serves this purpose. Inventories of employee characteristics can increase awareness of personnel inputs. Business firms can conduct educational programs on selected topics so that they will be more certain of employee knowledge and attitudes. Some of the research efforts that are directed toward identifying the nature of the organization's environment have as one of their goals the acquisition of knowledge about systems inputs. In fact, even moderately sophisticated organizations will allocate significant resources to make unknown inputs known.

The key to deciding whether to invest resources in discovering more about a given input is the perceived significance of that particular input for the total system. Does this particular input significantly affect the achievement of desired results? Sometimes this question is particularly difficult to answer because the secondary or tertiary effects of a given information flow through a system can be difficult to detect. For example, what difference does it make to corporate profits if 25 percent of the sales force are Marxists? Some people would maintain that such a large percentage of Marxists in the sales force completely disrupts the organization and leads to the demise of the system. Others might feel that the political and economic beliefs of salespersons are irrelevant to the profit position of the organization. In any case, it is difficult to collect and analyze the data required to make an objective determination of the interaction between Marxists in the sales force and corporate profits.

Consider the case of a large system such as a municipality and the difficulty of measuring the economic impact of additional industry. Yet the people who manage this system are constantly urged to develop policy relating to industrial growth. Assume for the moment that the desired result of city government is an enhanced quality of life. Given the present level of skill in measuring the effects of the behavior of governmental systems and the present inability to accurately predict the impact of any particular input on quality of life, the task of the manager of the city system is almost impossible. In fact, there is little agreement on the definition of quality of life, so how can the managers of cities be expected to improve it? The difficulty of the problem does not, however, diminish the need to know the nature of organizational inputs and their impact on the system.

Control of Inputs   After it is decided that a particular input is important, there is a desire to control the input in order to insure proper systems functioning. Some known inputs are controllable and some are not (see Figure 4-7).

Figure 4-7

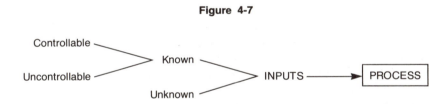

If the quality of water to be used in a particular manufacturing operation is important, the organization will certainly invest resources in order to know what the quality is. It is not adequate, however, just to know the quality; some effort must be made to control the quality, to insure that the quality stays within required limits or, at the very least, to insure that when the water is not within those limits, it is not used in the manufacturing operation.

There are several strategies that might be used to control the quality of the water. First, there could be an effort to control the quality at the source by only purchasing water that comes from a well, spring, or other source that provides the required quality. Second, there might be an effort to place responsibility for quality control on the supplier. In return for some reward, such as a premium price, the supplier can process the water in whatever way necessary to ensure proper quality. Third, the manufacturer might choose to do whatever is required within the system. This avoids paying the premium price to the supplier but involves the cost of the required water-processing system. Fourth, the manufacturer could seek some way to modify the manufacturing operation so that the available water will be satisfactory. This can require an investment in new operations.

Each of these four strategies has a cost to the system. Controlling input information flows is not free, and the cost of control must be weighed against the cost to the system if these flows are not controlled. Uncontrolled inputs reduce the probability that systems goals will be attained. Sometimes the reduction is so drastic that there is little choice but to try to control the information flow. At other times the reduction in the probability of goal attainment is so slight that it is negligible. In these cases it is foolish to invest resources in information flow control.

Sometimes the organization cannot control inputs because the knowledge required for control is not available to the system. The technology might not exist at all or it might not be readily available to the system at that particular time. The cost of acquiring knowledge must be carefully considered. Much of the investment in research can be considered an investment in input control. Consultants are sometimes hired to bring the knowledge required for input control into the system. A system might purchase patent rights in order to gain input control. Each of these strategies for gaining the knowledge required for input control involves an investment of organizational resources.

Of course the organization could know how to control a given information flow but not have the resources to invest in the control effort. For example, the system may know precisely how to process water so that it is satisfactory, but if equipment and personnel costs are so high that any anticipated profits would be consumed, it would not make sense to attempt the control effort. Alternatives must then be explored if the system is to operate effectively.

Systems inputs must be analyzed in terms of whether they are known or unknown and whether they are controlled or uncontrolled. Decisions about investments in increased understanding and control of systems inputs must be carefully considered because of the critical role that certain inputs play in systems functioning. It is neither reasonable nor possible to know or control all information flows into a system. Rather, there must be a careful attempt to identify the most critical information flows and concentrate organizational resources on these key elements.

Process

The fundamental task of all systems is to accomplish some functional information transformation, to move I_1 to I_2. This transformation is referred to as the process of a system. Understanding systems characteristics always involves the understanding of the process function, and the most obvious way to describe an organization is often in terms of its process. Several methods of grouping or classifying organizations have been developed as an aid in analysis. The most common is in terms of some description of the transformation itself.

Organizations may perform any one transformation or a combination of transformations: (1) The form, shape, or condition of the inputs may be changed, as is typically the case in a manufacturing firm, hospital, or school; (2) the arrangements or assortment of the inputs may be changed as occurs in a retail store when items purchased in large quantities are resold in smaller groupings or in a bank when the small savings of a large number of people are aggregated and loaned in much larger sums; (3) the place of the inputs may be changed, such as when a moving company takes furniture from one city to another, when a department store makes arrangements for goods to be brought from where they are in surplus to the location where they are needed, or when a welfare agency brings food and drugs into a disaster area. While it is not uncommon to find an organization that links several forms of transformation, one form will usually predominate and give the organization its chief characteristic.[5]

Considering process as a change in form, arrangement, or place is useful for an initial analysis but tends not to be useful for in-depth study of the relationship of the managerial function to the transformation process. Manufacturing firms, hospitals, and schools tend not to be managed in the same way. In fact, all manufacturing organizations are not similar in their structures. Other strategies for classifying organizations must be used if analysis is to be successful.

Process Elements   In an important study of industrial firms, Joan Woodward used three types of production systems to differentiate between manufacturing organizations.[6] They were: (1) unit and small-batch production, (2) large-batch, assembly, and mass production, and (3) process production. At this time it is not necessary to define the three types of organizational structures that correspond to these production systems, but it is important to note that Woodward's study showed that those firms with similar production technologies had similar organizational structures, even though they manufactured a wide range of products. The use of production systems as a means for classifying manufacturing organizations has proved to be very helpful in increasing the understanding of organizations.

The technology variable is only one dimension used in the literature to describe organizations and differentiate between them. For example, Charles Perrow[7] used the notion of a raw material variable. He maintained that technology varies along the dimensions of analyzable search to unanalyzable search and of few exceptions to many exceptions. Inputs of raw material variables vary along the dimensions of being well understood to not well understood and of being uniform and stable to nonuniform and unstable. Through the use of these two conceptualizations—the nature of the technology and the nature of the raw material—Perrow conceptualized various kinds of organizations and developed hypotheses about structure and management that have increased our ability to understand systems. Authors such as Woodward and Perrow point out the importance and value of looking at the success of the system that transforms I_1 (inputs) into I_2 (outputs).

It is a logical step from describing differences *between* organizations to describing variations *within* organizations. The various subunits within a system each have a distinct information processing function. The form of the subunit should be congruent with the function of the subunit rather than congruent with some master plan or overall systems form. Lorsch and Lawrence[8] conducted extensive research that shows that effective organizations are those that have attained a level of differentiation among the required transformation functions that is appropriate for each function. Effective organizations then achieve a sense of integration between functions in order to maintain the wholeness of the system.

As an example of process analysis in organizations, let us look at the organization as represented in Figure 4-8. Each of the subunits should be structured to facilitate the information transformation functions of that subunit. One would expect the organizational pattern for Personnel to be different from that for Industrial Engineering. Likewise, Marketing and Sales would be expected to have an organizational pattern different from Research and Development. The Plant Manager's organization will be different from Purchasing or Production Planning and Control. At the same time, these units must work with each of the other units, and there must be an integrating arrangement to facilitate the required information flows between them. Thus, there will be a procedure whereby the Plant Manager can inform Personnel of the need for certain kinds of workers and inform Purchasing of the need for certain materials. Marketing and Sales will have a procedure or structure for communicating customer preferences to Research and Development. Industrial Engineering must interface with both the Plant Manager and Production Planning and Control in order to facilitate the design of machine tools for the production process.

An understanding of this organization cannot be accomplished by simply knowing one ideal way to structure an organization. Each subunit must be understood in terms of its own information processing function. Consequently, there can be a highly decentralized Research and Development group and a highly centralized Quality Control group. Accounting will likely be more structured than Design Engineering. Purchasing and Personnel will have a kind of interaction with the outside environment different from Marketing and Sales or Research and Development. Each subunit must be organized in a way that promotes the accomplishment of a specific process function. However, not only must each subunit's pattern be understood, but the integrative links between subunits must be understood. How does Design Engineering exchange information with Research and Development? Through regularly scheduled meetings of supervisors? Through informed contact between technical people? Through formal directives? The nature of the organization is a function of the nature of these integrative functions *as well as* the nature of each subunit.

Figure 4-8.   Organization Chart

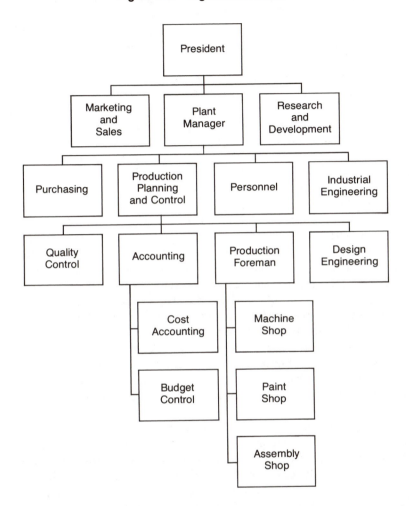

One way of assessing the task structure of the subunits and of the total firm is to look at each subunit's perception of its raw materials and at the nature of the technology used to transform these raw materials. Perrow's model would lead to the hypothesis that where the technology is characterized by an analyzable search procedure and where there are few exceptions to standard operating rules, the technology would be very routine, worker discretion would be low, coordination within groups would be by planning, and the system would be very formal and very centralized. Since it would be reasonable to suspect that the production operation in the firm would be routine, it could also be expected that the organization of the production function would be formal and centralized. Workers would have a low level of discretion and would work by following a detailed plan.

Because this organizational pattern is effective for the production unit, the unaware analyst might feel that other units should be organized in the same way. A look at the technological variable and the raw material variable for Research and Development would immediately cause this conclusion to be questioned. The technology of research and development is represented by an unanalyzable search process and by many exceptions. The raw materials are not well understood and are nonuniform and unstable. Therefore, this process is very nonroutine. Given this analysis, it would be expected that the research and development operation would provide for high worker discretion, coordination within groups would be accomplished by a review of results, relationships between workers would be informal, and power would be decentralized. Because of the differences in the information processing functions, organizations and subunits are expected to differ in their structure and management.

Although a research and development process would probably be structured differently from a production process, the production process itself must be examined for variables that account for organizational differences. Recall Woodward's classification of manufacturing systems as unit, mass, and process. Her research showed that structural variables such as length of line of command, span of control, and proportion of wage costs to total costs varied with the manufacturing technology. Therefore, it cannot be said that all production operations should have a long (or short) line of command; nor can it be said that the span of control should be narrow (or wide). Neither can a standard ratio of wage costs to total costs be set. The production process itself must be examined in light of the nature of the information transformations required, and the structure must be designed to match the process.

An understanding of the process function in systems must begin by looking at the differences in the fundamental information transformation functions. It is expected that those systems that process routine information will be significantly different from those that process nonroutine information, just as those that process nonroutine continuous information are expected to be significantly different from those that process nonroutine discontinuous information. The information selection and distortion characteristics of the processor are expected to contribute to the structural variables, and the interrelationships between information processors are expected to affect the way the overall process function is structured and managed.

Known and Unknown Processes   In addition to the basic nature of the process function, when examining systems processes, it must be recognized that some transformation functions are known and some are unknown (see Figure 4-9).

It is often possible to observe changes in an information flow and to be unaware of the specific processes that cause these changes. If the change is critical in terms of output goals, then the manager must invest resources to

Figure 4-9

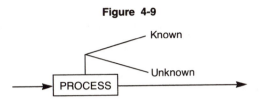

identify the cause of the change. If it is remembered that each information processor has its own unique selection and distortion characteristics, it is easy to understand the difficulty in trying to discover the full nature of the complex information processing that is likely to be occurring. This problem is complicated by the fact that each of the interactions between subunits is an opportunity for unplanned information processing to take place.

Many of the changes that take place in hospital patients are inexplicable in terms of any of the known information processing that takes place. Some people get well for unknown reasons; others die for unknown reasons. Most hospitals have relatively large subsystems that are committed to discovering unknown factors that affect patients. Hospitals also attempt to create systems so that they can know as much as possible about what happens to the patients. Despite this effort there is still much that happens that is a mystery to hospital staffs.

Most retail sales managers can easily describe many of the things that affect buyer behavior. Location and packaging of goods, price, usefulness, novelty, and convenience all play a role in shaping customer reaction to a product. At the same time, there are many unknown factors that influence customer behavior. These factors are a major cause of uncertainty in retail sales, and despite considerable effort, unexplained phenomena regularly occur in the retail industry.

Intended and Unintended Processes   Some of the known processing that takes place in a system is intended, but much of it is not (see Figure 4-10).

Figure 4-10

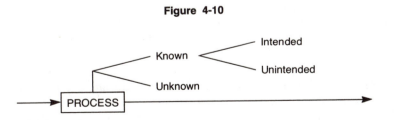

Often when a particular transformation is known, the assumption is that it was intended. There are, however, many cases in which known transformation functions are the result of unintended activity. One of the most famous cases is the discovery of penicillin. In the course of another experiment involving bacterial growth, Sir Alexander Fleming found mold growing in the culture. He soon noticed that the mold killed the bacteria, and from this he devised the set of experiments resulting in the discovery of penicillin. The processes of growing the mold and of killing the bacteria were known but unintended. When examining organizations it is important to be aware of unintended processes. Much of what occurs in organizations occurs by accident, and only the most naive observer would assume that all organizational processes are intended. Organizational energy is often spent discovering the nature of process activity and determining if unintended processes will interfere with the attainment of organizational goals.

Outputs

The purpose of the system is to generate some output or set of outputs that are usable by other systems in the environment. Without the generation of outputs the system has no function. It is the end product of the transformation $I_1 \longrightarrow I_2$ that is of major interest to most observers of systems behavior. Unless the outputs are useful, the system is not useful; therefore, systems analysis is particularly concerned with describing the information that flows from a system.

One must be careful not to confuse actual outputs with goals or desired outputs. Actual outputs are almost always at variance to some degree with desired outputs. While goals or desired outputs are of interest to the systems analyst, it is the actual output of the system that is of primary concern.

The outputs of a system are a function of the nature of the inputs and the nature of the transformation processes. Changes in either input or processor will result in changes in the output.

Known and Unknown Outputs   If there was perfect knowledge of the inputs and processes of a system, then it would be possible to predict the outputs of the system perfectly. However, it should be recalled that there are unknown processes and unknown inputs in the system, and therefore it is not possible to have perfect knowledge about the outputs of a system. Thus, there are both known outputs and unknown outputs.

Figure 4-11 illustrates the concept of known and unknown outputs from a system. Much organizational effort is spent in attempting to identify the various outputs. For example, an organization may be concerned about its public image. It may hire a public relations firm to study attitudes and beliefs of people about the organization. This is an effort to move certain unknown outputs into the known category. Another example is the inspection of assembled parts leaving an assembly line. There is an effort here to make sure that the quality of the output is known by the organization.

Figure 4-11

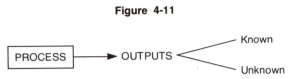

Another example of an effort to know the nature of the outputs of a system is through surveys of users of a product taken some time after the product has left the system. It is the purpose of such surveys to discover characteristics of the output that could not be discovered at the time that it was produced.

Anticipated and Unanticipated Outputs   Some known outputs are anticipated and some are unanticipated. The organization has been created to produce certain known outputs, but in the process of producing those, there will be other outputs that are known but were not anticipated in systems design. Managers might well anticipate that a particular set of work rules will improve worker performance, but they might not anticipate that these same work rules would increase the workers' interest in joining a union. Failure to anticipate this outcome might create many problems for the organization. Therefore, managers try to anticipate the complete range of systems outputs, but they are aware of the fact that the imperfection of their own knowledge of the system means that there will be unanticipated outputs.

Figure 4-12

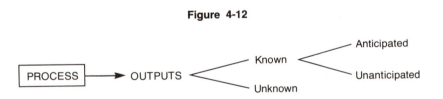

Figure 4-12 illustrates this concept. Certain known systems outputs are anticipated and some are unanticipated. Some of the unanticipated outputs might be extremely valuable to the company. For example, many manufacturing organizations have found that materials that had been scrapped became profitable because of the development of a new technology by another organization. The unanticipated output in this example is profit from the scrap materials from a given process function. The organization that is constantly thinking about its outputs and attempting to understand them is often able to turn an unanticipated output into a profitable situation for the organization.

The analyst must keep in mind that the desired results or goals of the system are a great influence on systems behavior but are not the same as the actual outputs of the system. The analyst is concerned not only about

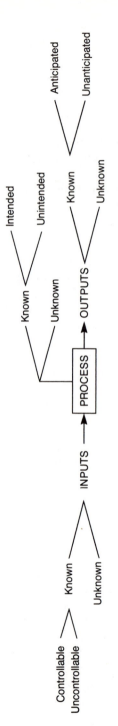

Figure 4-13

these intended or desired outputs but also about the actual outputs and about the impact of those outputs on other systems in the environment. If the outputs of a system that are known and anticipated are congruent with the system's desired goals, then it is likely that those who control the resources to determine whether the system will continue to function will provide those resources. However, if unknown or unanticipated outputs affect the environment in such a way as to cause a response from the environment, such as pollution, it is possible that the system will have to cease functioning. The analyst is concerned with the overview of systems outputs and with understanding how these outputs interact with the system's environment.

Summary

We have expanded our base notion of a system by attempting to describe some of the characteristics of the systems inputs, processes, and outputs. Figure 4-13 represents an expanded diagram of the basic system.

Notes

[1] R. L. Ackoff, "Toward a System of Systems Concepts," *Management Science,* July 1971, p. 661.

[2] Kenyon B. De Greene, *Sociotechnical Systems: Factors in Analysis, Design and Management* (Englewood Cliffs, N.J.: Prentice-Hall, 1973), p. 4.

[3] Frank J. Clark, Ronald Gale, and Robert Gray, *Business Systems and Data Processing Procedures* (Englewood Cliffs, N.J.: Prentice-Hall, 1972), p. 37.

[4] De Greene, *Sociotechnical Systems,* p. 12.

[5] Joseph A. Litterer, *The Analysis of Organizations,* 2nd ed. (New York: Wiley, 1973). Used by permission.

[6] J. Woodward, *Industrial Organization: Theory and Practice* (Oxford University Press: London, 1965).

[7] Charles Perrow, *Organizational Analysis: A Sociological View* (Belmont, Calif.: Brooks/Cole, 1970).

[8] Jay W. Lorsch and Paul R. Lawrence, *Organization Planning: Cases and Concepts* (Homewood, Ill.: Irwin, 1972).

Planning and Control in Open Systems

5

Introduction

If systems were perfect and all inputs were known and controllable, all processes known and intended, and no selection and distortion took place, then all outputs would be known and anticipated, and the system could be permitted to run with no mechanism to monitor its behavior. However, no system is perfect. Workers misinterpret instructions; machines wear out; raw materials are contaminated by chemicals in the air; all manner of things go wrong and cause the organization not to perform as intended. Because of this, all systems need to look at their actual outputs and compare them with intended outputs. This comparison is accomplished through the use of feedback loops in the system.

Systems also are continually looking to the future to model changes in the inputs or processes to determine if the altered output would be desired. Even the sole proprietor of a small variety store has a model of the store in mind and mulls over how changing the goods that are carried or the display arrangement or newspaper advertising will alter sales and profits. Planning is looking into the future to anticipate the output of adjustments in inputs or processes.

Feedback

In a feedback loop, information that is part of the systems output is returned to the system as input and is used to compare the present state of the system to the desired state of the system. This particular information flow is called feedback. As stated earlier, Clark, Gale, and Gray defined feedback as "that function of the system which automatically brings back information about a situation under consideration to the source of that in-information."[1] Systems feedback is extremely important because it is through the monitoring of the feedback in a system that the organization is able to make judgments about the system's state and about its level of performance.

A fundamental part of the feedback loop for a system is the model that acts as a comparator. This model is used to compare the actual output information from a system with the intended output information from that system. The relationship of that model to the system is shown in Figure 5-1. As Figure 5-1 shows, information is taken from the output of the system and run through a comparator model to compare actual outputs with desired outputs.

Figure 5-1

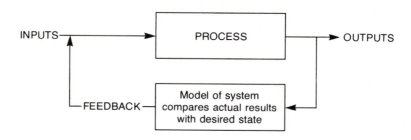

These comparator models can be very formal. Formal models are those in which the relationship between the model elements is understood and defined. For example, mathematical equations are formal models. Examples of formal models that are used in feedback systems include accounting controls, profit and loss statements, geographical analyses of sales, analysis of purchase price variance, analysis of materials usage variance, plant performance reports, reports of selling expenses by salesmen, and balance sheets. Each of these is a formal model utilized to compare the actual outputs of the system with the intended outputs.

There are many informal models used by organizations to get feedback about the performance of systems. These informal models represent important sources of information, but the relationship between the elements within the models normally cannot be specified and, in fact, may be situation-specific. Examples of informal models that are utilized in a feedback system include unorganized customer complaints, information gathered informally from suppliers, casual observations by managers as they move around the organization, and indications of organizational performance gathered from informal personal relationships within the organization.

The management of formal models that are used for feedback is comparatively simple. It involves the understanding of the kind of information necessary to evaluate the performance of the system and to determine whether the actual results are the same as the desired results. Informal models for feedback often create difficult problems for the organization. This is due in part to the fact that much of the information in the informal feedback model will be considered nonroutine by the organization and therefore be difficult to process. In any case, the organization must use both formal and informal models for comparing actual outputs with intended outputs in order to achieve its objectives.

Output Measures

The measurement of systems outputs is frequently difficult. When it is possible, the organization attempts to make a direct measurement of actual systems outputs and then compares these directly with the intended outputs. For example, the organization would like to know exactly how many products are produced in a given day and then compare the actual number produced with the production schedule. Another example of direct measurement is to look at the cash balance at the end of any given fiscal period and compare it with the intended cash balance.

Because of the nature of measurement itself, it is sometimes necessary that particular desired outputs be indirectly measured. Some of the output of a system is very difficult to measure and to compare with a desired state. For example, if the desired output in a class on music appreciation is an increased liking for classical music, it might be difficult to measure whether students have achieved this goal. In particular, it might be difficult to know whether to attribute any change in that particular characteristic to the organization. For this reason the teacher is often required to attempt to measure indirectly whether students have increased their liking for classical music, such as by attempting to measure how much the students have learned about classical music. This might be done despite the fact that there is no direct, demonstrable correlation between knowledge about classical music and appreciation for classical music. It is, however, so much simpler to measure knowledge about classical music than to measure appreciation.

One of the ways to increase greatly the effectiveness of both direct and indirect measurements in a feedback system is to use statistical techniques. Both descriptive statistics and inferential statistics are useful tools in the development of formal models for feedback systems. Descriptive statistics allow phenomena to be described in a way that makes comparisons between various descriptions possible. For example, determining the average life of a light bulb made by a given process, a descriptive statistic, allows a comparison of the effectiveness of one process with another. Inferential statistics permit inferences about a relationship between two phenomena.

For example, whether knowledge learned about classical music implies appreciation of classical music could be tested by using inferential statistics to determine the correlation between a person's knowledge of classical music and that person's appreciation of classical music.

It would be helpful if all the output information from a given system could be compared to a desired result. This, of course, is impossible. One reason is that many of the measures utilized to make such comparisons effectively destroy the information. For example, to find out what the strength of a machine screw is generally requires destructive testing. Obviously, a manufacturer of machine screws would not choose to destructively test all products because then there would be nothing to sell. Instead, a sampling technique is used, by which it is possible for a system to determine with a relatively high degree of accuracy what the comparison is between the actual output and the desired output without comparing all of the information that flows out of the system.

Negative and Positive Feedback Loops

The feedback system should be as carefully designed as the larger system itself. A model, either formal or informal, must be developed and choices must be made about whether direct or indirect measurements ought to be used, whether statistical strategies ought to be used, whether they should be descriptive or inferential, whether population measurement should be engaged in, and whether sampling can be done. A design of the feedback system is a function of the available technology and the complexity of the output being monitored. Organizations invest considerable resources in feedback systems in order to affirm the attainment of organizational goals. Information in the feedback loop causes changes in systems performance as the system continually adjusts and takes corrective action necessary to reduce deviations from the desired course. Some feedback is such that it reduces the deviations of the output from a steady state. This is termed *negative feedback*. Other feedback increases deviations of the output from a steady state.[2] This is termed *positive feedback*. Positive feedback usually leads to instability in the system, while negative feedback is used to provide stability.[3] Negative feedback is generally associated with self-regulation and goal direction, while positive feedback is associated with growth and decay.[4]

In general, the system fares better if the feedback is negative. The information flow should be such that the system becomes more stable over time. Organizations seek feedback about the quality of their products. If the information flow in the feedback loop indicates unacceptable deviations from standards, corrective action is taken that brings product quality back into an acceptable range. In this case, the organization has received negative feedback that has acted to bring the system back into a steady state.

Suppose, however, that the organization receives information that sales are down, and the reaction is to raise prices in order to maintain the incoming revenue required to meet fixed costs. This increase in price creates a further decline in sales with a subsequent decrease in revenue. The response is another round of price increases in the attempt to deter sliding revenue, but demand continues to slide. The organization is caught in a spiral of instability caused by a positive feedback loop. Unless this loop and its effects can be broken, the system will self-destruct.

There are some cases in which a positive feedback loop can be good for a system and a negative loop bad. An increase in promotional efforts for a product can result in an increase in demand, generating more orders for production, followed by a subsequent increase in shipments and revenue, which in turn provides more resources to be spent on promotional efforts, which generate still more orders, and so on. Here is a positive feedback loop that is good for the organization. Suppose that the increased demand resulting in increased order rates had created a large order backlog rather than an increase in shipments. This would have led to an increase in delivery time, which tends to decrease demand. This is a nonreinforcing effect and the feedback loop is negative. The result of this situation may be detrimental.

The general observation still holds that positive feedback is usually dysfunctional for systems, and negative feedback usually functional. Organizations must understand the effects of feedback loops and attempt to utilize all types of feedback to move toward their goals.[5]

Control

Feedback systems are primarily utilized to control system behavior. *Control* is the use of feedback loops to identify and correct deviations from desired systems behavior. Because the organization is concerned with goal attainment, a great deal of time is spent developing and monitoring control systems. Examples of such control systems are accounting policies and procedures and inventory control processes.

The chief characteristic of control functions is their tendency to isolate only certain crucial elements for attention. The complexity of the information and the information processors prohibits equal attention to all elements at one time. Organizations deal with this problem through both the isolation of functions to be controlled and the sequential attention to various elements. One example of the limited nature of control is the control function in an automobile. The basic feedback systems include a speedometer and a gas gauge. Other malfunction possibilities are not usually monitored directly and continuously. It is felt that most other possible malfunctions will be related to a loss of performance along one of these dimensions or will cause the information processor to cease functioning completely;

this would lead to search behavior beyond the evidence presented by the standard feedback systems.

A second characteristic of control functions is the absorption of considerable organizational energy without providing a clear return on the investment. This often leads to attempts to simplify the control function, and these attempts can lead to a *lack* of control that is not immediately apparent. The question then revolves around what the trade-offs between energy savings are and what would be the potential failure due to lack of control. Attempts to reduce inspection costs through the use of statistical sampling techniques represent one effort to resolve such trade-off problems. The use of random spot audit of the accounting process is another example.

Control Systems Evaluation

Because of the importance of control functions and feedback systems to organizations, it is useful to have guidelines to evaluate control systems, even though many considerations must be situation-specific.

Guidelines for Evaluation of Control Systems

1. Time lag between output and comparison should be brief.

2. Increases in measurement efforts should increase movement toward goal attainment.

3. Systems goals that are to be controlled should be well defined.

4. Excess information should not be generated in the control process. (Avoid information overload.)

5. Control efforts should give a good systems overview; they should give a realistic perspective of systems behavior.

6. Control efforts should be limited to areas that management can change. (For example, monitor what and how employees are paid but not how they spend what they make.)

7. Theoretically, the control system should report only things that are wrong within the system. Practically, the control system should report as little routine information as possible.

8. The control system should enable the entire system to improve control functions over time.

9. The control system should not cost more to the overall system than the error that it averts would cost. (Inspection costs should be based on costs generated by returns, warranties, and market loss caused by customer dissatisfaction if there was no inspection.)

10. There is always a social exchange within the system; those monitored should not be antagonized by the control system.

11. The control system should be accurate, reliable, valid, and independent.

12. The control system should be sensitive and diagnostic.

13. The control system should be adaptable; if the system is changed, the control system should still function.

14. The control system should be autonomous and have the ability to see problems and correct the deviations.

15. Ideally, the control system should control only and not manage. If it does manage, it contaminates the system. (For example, a program manager for a project should not at the same time serve as the project evaluator. Each task conflicts with the other one.)

16. The control system should regulate the system without outside information. It should:

  a. tell if something is wrong and what is wrong

  b. diagnose, that is, tell what causes the deviation

  c. regulate, that is, trigger corrective changes

  The complexity increases from 16a to 16c.

Control mechanisms and feedback systems are fundamental to understanding systems in general because of the important role they play in maintaining systems stability and in assisting the organization in achieving its goals.

Feedforward

All organizations have the capacity to look to the future and to anticipate what the future state of the system is going to be given the nature of critical input variables and the nature of the environment. This is necessary so that the system can anticipate adjustments. It is also necessary so that the system can determine the probability of meeting goals. All systems, therefore, have feedforward loops that provide information on expectations of future behavior.[6] Feedforward loops identify critical input variables and run this information through a simulator of the process function. The outputs of the simulator are then compared with the intended outputs of the system to enable the organization to anticipate whether the process function will achieve organizational goals.

Figure 5-2 illustrates the simulator model and its relationship to the system. It shows that the feedforward loop is a method whereby various inputs, labeled I_1^1 through I_1^n can be run through various processes, labeled P^1 through P^n in order to get outputs I_2^1 through I_2^n. The input and process functions of the simulator represent approximations of the critical information that would flow through the system and also of the transformation processes that would operate on that critical information. I_2^1 through I_2^n represent the variety of outputs that might occur as a result of different combinations of inputs and processes. The organization then looks at the various outputs, $I_2{}^1$ through $I_2{}^n$, and decides which of these is closest to the desired output of the system. Then the particular combination of inputs and processes used to achieve the most desired output will be used.

Figure 5-2

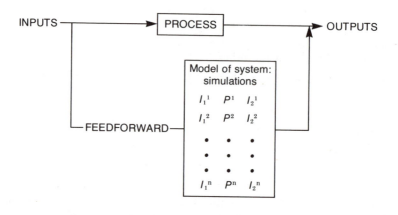

Simulator Models

Simulator models can be extremely formal and extremely complex. Linear programming can be used to determine alternatives for achieving a goal or desired result within resource constraints (on a cost-effective basis). For example, different grades of gasoline are obtained by combining certain blending gasolines that are the direct output of the refinery operation. In an actual refinery operation there are many blending gasolines, many final-product gasolines (for example, various grades of aviation and motor gasoline), and many characteristics that are considered important in the chemical composition of the various grades of gasoline (including, for example, octane rating, vapor pressure, sulfur content, and gum content). The assumption in this simplified example is that a refinery has available only two types of blending gasoline.

Characteristics of Blending Gasoline

	Octane Rating	Vapor Pressure	Amount Available (in barrels)
Type 1	104	4	30,000
Type 2	94	9	70,000

These blending gasolines can be mixed to produce two final products, Hi Flyer and Auto Run.

Characteristics of Final-Product Gasoline

	Minimum Octane Rating	Maximum Vapor Pressure	Maximum Sales (in barrels)	Selling Price (per barrel)
Hi Flyer	102	5	70,000	$17.90
Auto Run	96	8	unlimited	$20.00

Based on the sales expectations for Auto Run, management decides to produce it exclusively instead of continuing to produce both Hi Flyer and Auto Run.

Thus, feedforward loops provide the organization with a mechanism for evaluating current policies and procedures in light of forecasts of future environments and its current operations. The gasoline manufacturer in the previous example has changed product policy: The company will begin to provide only one gasoline product, Auto Run. Plans will now need to be made for converting Hi Flyer production facilities into Auto Run facilities.

Another example of formal simulator models are pilot programs organized to test the impact of certain organizational policies. For example, a company that wishes to determine whether a change in product design will be favorably received by customers will run a pilot study testing customer reaction to the change. The sample of customers to be used for the test is carefully selected to represent the typical market for the product. The reactions of the customers to the test product are recorded and adjustments made to the product design where indicated. As a result of this pilot program, the company then can decide whether to go ahead with a major change in its product design.

All formal simulator models do not necessarily reflect accurately the actual behavior of the system. For example, a particular change in product design that appears to be extremely successful in a pilot program could fail when tested in the general market. It is therefore necessary to consider trade-offs of time and cost with perceived accuracy. The formal model should represent closely the actual system in order that the outputs of the model will reflect the outputs of the system.

Informal models are also used for simulating future states of a system. One of the purposes of planning meetings is to try out various ideas for different procedures with a group of managers and/or experts in order to get an informal reading of how those ideas might work out in practice. An organization might assemble its executive staff to discuss the impact of relocating from one section of the country to another. Various members of the executive staff will be expected to bring their expertise to bear on this problem and to make projections or suggestions about the impact of the organizational move.

Often managers in an organization will ask workers "what if" questions in an effort to utilize the workers' experience to develop a simulator model of a new situation. For example, a foreman might ask a machinist what would happen *if* the material used to make a particular part was changed from aluminum to magnesium. A good machinist would then be able to tell the foreman the difficulties that would arise in the metal-working process and the advantages that might accrue in the production process. In fact, the worker might even suggest changes in the process that would alleviate or remove some of the difficulties created by the change in input. In this way the foreman has essentially been building a feedforward model to anticipate the outputs of a change in the input and/or process.

Forecasting

One of the major requirements for building simulator models is the ability to forecast. Forecasting can be done in several ways. One way is trend analysis; in trend analysis it is the expectation that the near future will be like the near past. If it is possible to collect information about the near past, then there can be considerable understanding of the near future. For example, if a company says that over the past five years it has been growing at an annual rate of 5 percent and therefore it anticipates that it will continue to grow at the same rate over the next five years, it is using trend analysis.

Somewhat similar is the notion of projection. A projection is made when an organization assumes certain environmental changes as it looks to the future. The assumption here is not that a trend from the near past will be followed but that new environmental forces and new organizational forces will alter the existing trend. Based on the past impact of similar environmental or organizational forces, the organization can predict the degree of the shift from past trends. Projection is based on knowledge of a previous condition, but a continuation of the near past trend is not assumed.

Another way to make forecasts is with expert opinion or expert guesses. People who have had considerable experience with a phenomenon or a given set of phenomena can be asked to make a forecast based on their knowledge. In many cases a medical prognosis is essentially an expert guess about the future condition of a patient given a particular treatment program.

It is extremely difficult to make forecasts for organizations that exist in a complex interactive environment. Many useful mathematical and analytical techniques for forecasting were developed with the advent of highly complex information processing computer systems. But it must be realized that the future is in part a function of what other systems in the environment do relative to the organization. It is the unpredictability of environmental factors that creates difficulty in forecasting. However, in order to have a useful feedforward model, it is necessary for the system to develop the capacity to forecast with reasonable accuracy.

Critical information is run through the feedforward loop and through the simulator model so that the outputs of the simulator can be compared with the desired outputs of the processor. In addition to forecasting being important in determining the accuracy of this comparison, the accuracy depends on the ability of the organization to create simulators that accurately model the processor. Refer back to Figure 5-2, where the model of the system is expected to simulate the behavior of the system. One might have, for example, an excellent pilot project that produces outputs that are exactly what the organization wants. But the pilot project may not represent the systems process, so that when the system is activated using the information gathered from the pilot program, the outputs of the system are not the same as those of the pilot. Often the difference between simulator behavior and processor behavior is a function of the organization's inability to create useful and accurate simulators. For example, if a refinery process that is modeled through a series of mathematical equations is to be a useful simulator, then the mathematical equation must accurately represent the behavior of the oil refinery. There will almost always be certain variables that cannot be taken into account by the mathematical equations. If, for example, the workers go on strike and thus shut the refinery down, the output of the refinery process will not be the same as that predicted by the simulator.

Planning

It can be noted from this discussion that feedforward is related to the future state of affairs for the system. Therefore, it should come as no surprise that the planning process in organizations is closely related to and relies on the feedforward loop. *Planning* is the use of feedforward loops to make decisions concerning the future behavior of the system. The planning process is no better than the ability of the system to identify critical information, to build simulators that accurately reflect the process functions, and to compare the output of the simulator with the desired result of the system.

Planning is critical to the successful operation of organizations. The ability of the organization to anticipate the future and to make adjustments in the present in order to cope successfully with future conditions is necessary for organizational survival. Because of the importance of planning functions and feedforward systems in organizations, it is necessary for managers to develop ways to evaluate their planning systems.

Guidelines to Evaluate Planning Systems

As in the case of control systems, many of the guidelines for evaluating planning systems are situation-specific. But there are some general guidelines that we wish to propose as helpful in analyzing organizational behavior.

Guidelines for Evaluation of Planning Systems

1. The time frame must be relevant.

    a. The time frame for the plan development should not exceed the life of the problem or project under study.

    b. The time frame of the plan itself should not exceed the life of the problem or project under study.

2. Cost of planning must be less than the benefit of planning.

3. Knowledge of goals and constraints is necessary.

4. The planning system must serve as a critical way to try to manage the future.

5. The planning system must act like the system, whereas the control system is involved only in a comparison.

6. The planning system must measure the value of critical inputs as well as define them.

7. The system should have great flexibility. It should define multiple alternatives and simulate the effects of these alternatives under multiple conditions of the critical input variables. For example, the planning process for a community's water supply should include the simulation of multiple alternatives, such as desalinization plants, river sources, and aquifer sources. Service needs under each alternative should be simulated at different levels of the critical variables, such as population, density of development, consumption per capita, and water quality.

8. The simulation should permit the planner to maximize net social benefit (or net private benefit).

9. The simulator's outputs must be believable. For example, the operations research staff must be able to convince management of the validity of the simulator's outputs.

10. Simplifying assumptions must be made and stated explicitly.

11. The planning system should simulate total systems output in at least one of the following three ways:

    a. It should simulate maximum output with a given amount of resources or a given level of output with minimum resources.

    b. It should simulate expected values of outcomes with a given level of resources. The expected values of an outcome are found by multiplying each possible level of the outcome by the probability of that outcome level (where the sum of probabilities equals 1.0) and summing these products. That is,

$$\text{expected value} \;=\; \sum_{j=1}^{n} R_j\, P_j,$$

where R_j = a given value of a certain outcome and P_j = the probability of R_j's occurrence.

c. It should simulate the organization as the organization now is, and it should have the capacity to simulate the organization as the organization could be with new organizational resources or environmental changes.

12. Critical variables should include at least these elements: powers of negotiators and other political factors, resources and their quantities used in the transformation process, and sensitivity of the critical variables.

13. Outputs of the simulator should be measured in multiple ways to reflect multiple objectives and to minimize the distortion in the interpretation of outcomes. For example, public education output measurements should include evaluation of several skill changes—reading comprehension, reading speed, social skills, mathematical skills, and so on—rather than reading comprehension alone.

14. Ideally the simulation should be complete and exhaustive; it should consider all the variables in the system and all interactions. Practically, the simulation can only deal with a limited number of variables. Thus, the critical variables must approximate the whole.

15. Simulations should be continuously updated with changes in the levels or impacts of critical variables on systems objectives.

16. The simulation should estimate the levels of undesired outputs. For example, the introduction of new technology might change employee morale.

Planning through the use of feedforward systems is fundamental to the understanding of systems in general and to the understanding of organizations. It is through the successful management of planning and feedforward systems that organizations maintain viability and have some potential for directing their efforts to achieve organizational goals.

Open Systems

An open system is a system that engages in information exchanges with the environment. All organizations are open systems because all have significant information exchanges with the environment that influence their behavior and the behavior of their subsystems. The fact that organizations are open systems is extremely important.

The interaction that takes place between the organization and the environment results in the impact of one upon the other. To understand the organization requires an understanding of this interaction. For example, English professors affect the environment by training almost all public school English teachers. Managers, in this case English professors, can fail to see the relation between the action and reaction of the organization and its environment. The quality of writing of college students is to some degree the result of the work of English professors who train public school English teachers. This is an action-reaction system.

The task environment of the organization is composed of elements and information with varying degrees of importance. Some of the information in the environment is very important to the functioning of the organization and some is not. The specific information that is important to an organization can change over time. The organization must be aware of information in the environment that is important to organizational functioning and of information that is not important. Again, an example will be helpful. Most organizations were not particularly concerned about the cost of energy prior to the Middle East embargo of 1973 because until that time energy was cheap for most organizations. However, since the 1973 embargo, all organizations have been much more sensitive to the cost of energy as they plan their organizational strategies.

The information exchange between the organization and the environment varies between the organization giving more information to the environment than it takes in to receiving more information than it gives out. Over time the organization cannot afford to give more information to the environment than it receives. There are times when the organization is seeking information because it has an inadequate information level, and there are other times when the organization is discharging information because it has essentially too much information. For example, with high inventory levels of fresh produce in a restaurant, an appropriate organizational response might be to give unusually large portions to customers. With low inventory levels an appropriate response might be to decrease portion sizes or offer substitutions.

Organizational flexibility is the ability of the organization to shift with changes in environmental information inputs. Organizational rigidity is the ability of the organization to resist environmental influences. A system can be either flexible or rigid in dealing with changes in the information flows from the environment. This involves a choice of organizational strategy for dealing with environmental change. Neither a flexible nor a rigid strategy guarantees organizational success. Under some conditions the ability of the organization to resist changing because of environmental influences can be the ability that permits the organization to survive in the face of a variable environment. Nevertheless, a certain degree of flexibility is normally required for any organization to survive over long periods of time. The U.S. railroads, because they felt that their position in the transportation industry was not threatened, did not develop a flexible response system to changing transportation preferences. This rigidity has made it difficult for the railroads to reach goal attainment.

In the face of environmental changes and the sometimes natural responses to be either more flexible or more rigid, organizations must maintain internal stability. By internal stability is meant maintenance of the integrity of or consistency in the relationship of the parts of the organization; if the integrity is not maintained, the character of the organization will be completely changed. For example, if a college begins to admit students who have not graduated from high school because fewer students are

Figure 5-3.   Types of Interaction Between the Environment and the Organization

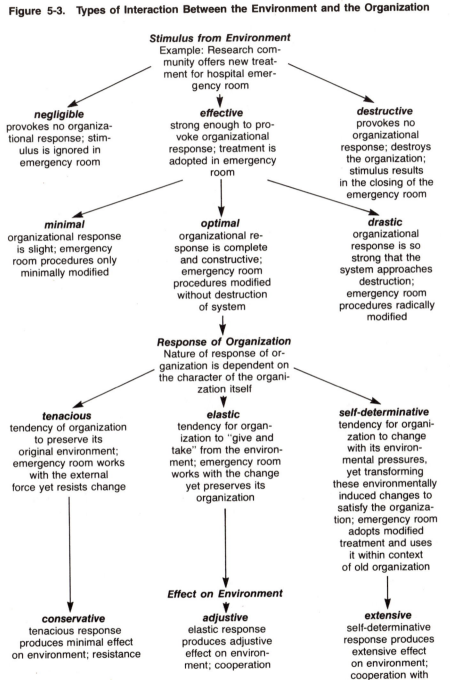

Stimulus from Environment
Example: Research community offers new treatment for hospital emergency room

negligible
provokes no organizational response; stimulus is ignored in emergency room

effective
strong enough to provoke organizational response; treatment is adopted in emergency room

destructive
provokes no organizational response; destroys the organization; stimulus results in the closing of the emergency room

minimal
organizational response is slight; emergency room procedures only minimally modified

optimal
organizational response is complete and constructive; emergency room procedures modified without destruction of system

drastic
organizational response is so strong that the system approaches destruction; emergency room procedures radically modified

Response of Organization
Nature of response of organization is dependent on the character of the organization itself

tenacious
tendency of organization to preserve its original environment; emergency room works with the external force yet resists change

elastic
tendency for organization to "give and take" from the environment; emergency room works with the change yet preserves its organization

self-determinative
tendency for organization to change with its environmental pressures, yet transforming these environmentally induced changes to satisfy the organization; emergency room adopts modified treatment and uses it within context of old organization

Effect on Environment

conservative
tenacious response produces minimal effect on environment; resistance

adjustive
elastic response produces adjustive effect on environment; cooperation

extensive
self-determinative response produces extensive effect on environment; cooperation with greater perception on how the organization interacts with the environment

graduating from high school, then the college will lose its character and integrity and become an unstable organization. If a production operation attempts to accommodate too wide a range of variability in the raw materials used for production, then the organization will become unstable and be unable to produce quality products and thus meet its organizational goals. Management must be concerned with a stabilization strategy to face changing environmental conditions.

There are a number of possible types of interaction between the environment and the organization, which are illustrated in Figure 5-3.[7] This figure illustrates the variety of ways in which a system can respond to changes in the environment.

Characteristics of Open Systems

There are certain common characteristics of open systems that must be understood in order to understand the nature of organizations. The following characteristics of open systems have been adapted from Katz and Kahn's analysis.[8]

Characteristics of Open Systems

1. Open systems import energy and information from the environment.

2. Open systems involve a transformation process that entails the change of information from a given state to another.

3. Open systems have an output of information (such as energy or heat loss) into the environment.

4. Open systems are characterized by cycles of events. Systems activity is not represented by a straight line (———————) but by a cycle ($\sim$). These cycles are convenient tools whereby systems can be conceptually bounded. Thus, where repetition begins is the end of the cycle. Individual human behavior is fairly cyclic from 8 a.m. to 8 a.m. and can be seen as a system. Within this twenty-four-hour cycle are numerous other subsystems, such as fixing and consuming breakfast from 8 a.m. to 8:30 a.m.

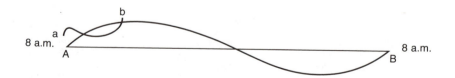

A ($\sim$) B = one cycle within the system

a ($\sim$) b = one cycle of a subsystem within the system

A warehouse is another example of a system easily bounded by a cyclic approach. The cycle begins with an input of inventory purchases and ends with an output of materials leaving inventory. Somewhere within the system the inventory must be processed to analyze the coming and going of goods. There must also be a feedback system to determine if outflow is reasonable given the inflow. The traditional linear approach to organizational analysis sees cyclic performance of the system as error or fluctuations from the norm. This variation is very expensive to reduce and can never be entirely removed. A manager has to determine what level of error or variation is acceptable.

Reading the cycle can be very complicated. The cycle must be sampled carefully to get a true picture of the trend. If the cycle is repeatedly monitored at point E, the direction of the organization is seen as down when in effect the trend of the organization is level.

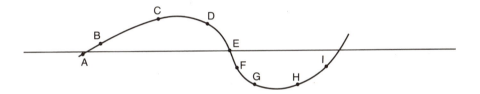

Incorrect evaluation of systems direction leads to a pendulum effect, where the managerial corrective action is overreactive and throws the system off the desired direction. An example of cyclic behavior is office morale. A steady state of morale is not feasible; there will be days of high and low morale in a normal office. Management needs to realize the trend of the office morale and take appropriate corrective actions if the trend is unacceptable. Only when the trend is understood can management initiate appropriate responses.

Cyclic behavior within systems thinking is becoming increasingly important. Evaluations (such as employee evaluations) depend on grasping the trend of a system rather than its position at one point in time.

Cycles can assume different shapes. A product life cycle or the life cycle of a tool bit may be represented as follows:

This shows that product usefulness is at first negligible, then rises, peaks, and if use is continued, becomes counterproductive. Understanding the shape of the cycle can improve managerial efficiency. If the tool bit is routinely removed from production at the end of a normal span of productive performance, waste of materials and man hours is minimized. Similarly, daily replacement of operating room light bulbs may be reasonable to prevent surgery interruption; daily replacement of office lights is probably an unreasonable expense.

The length of the systems cycle can create managerial problems. The cycle can last longer than the manager's career. Increasingly, managers are mobile and move to new positions before even relatively short cycles can repeat. With highly mobile managers the system can be manipulated to show good performance temporarily. But in the long run the managerial action that looked good in the short run will jeopardize later systems performance, perhaps after the manager has moved into a new position.

a (—►) b = one manager's time frame within a system's cycle

5. Open systems are characterized by negative entropy. This is the ability to utilize resources from the environment to maintain a sense of order in systems structure. Energy from the environment is stored by the system and used to resist the natural tendency of any system to move toward a random structure. While negative entropy is an abstract concept, the following three examples will illustrate it. First, organizations as open systems are able to use organizational slack or excess organizational resources to maintain the sense of structure and order of the system. Second, the employees of an organization bring many skills and experiences normally unused in their jobs. However, when a crisis arises, these skills and experiences are available and can contribute to maintaining the structure and order of the system. Third, in a similar fashion, organizations are able to obtain technology from the environment to maintain systems order and structure.

6. A system must have the ability to observe, compare, and correct its state. Negative feedback serves this function. Negative feedback draws a system toward a desired direction. If a system is moving upward and the desired direction is level, appropriate corrective action could be downward. However, the corrective action could lead to a new, improper downward direction. Again corrective action is needed.

corrective action taken

desired direction

Systems must have a capacity to regulate their activities. Much of the energy of the organization is spent resisting change because it tries to maintain a sense of stability. The desired state of the organization is not always the same as the steady state. The human body steady state is 98.6° F, but with certain medical conditions, such as hemorrhage, a lower body temperature is the desired state. External forces such as ice packs are imposed on the system to reach the desired state, yet the organism continues efforts to move toward the steady state.

Negative feedback is made possible via energy derived from negative entropy. Without negative feedback the system would not be cyclic but degenerative. To the degree that an organization can routinize, it can function with less negative entropy. The manager strives to create a system that can be readily monitored for appropriate corrective action and not be subject to shock.

7. Dynamic homeostasis is the preservation of the character of the system; the system strives to maintain its integrity. The difficulty that an airplane manufacturer would find in adding an automobile to its production capability illustrates the resistance of the system to changes in its character.

8. Over time, open systems become more specialized and increasingly differentiated. There are limits to the complexity attainable, but these limits can be relaxed with increasing technology. People naturally tend to take on specialized roles unless a manager interferes. This movement toward specialization is a part of the growth phenomenon. The introduction of professionals with a limited focus (such as criminal lawyers and environmental lawyers) illustrates differentiation. Lorsch and Lawrence found that the most successful companies have attained a level of differentiation appropriate to the complexity of the task environment. Less successful companies seek some normative state rather than an appropriately differentiated state.[9]

9. Integration is required to keep the system together, as over time the system becomes increasingly differentiated. For example, the Medicaid program provides services for the elderly ranging from home-based custodial care for patients to care in nursing homes with twenty-four-hour skilled nursing services available that are similar to hospital services. For optimal service for the aged, all levels of care need to be vertically integrated, yet extreme differentiation in the types of service provided makes integration difficult. A choice must be made between a management model that emphasizes home care and one that emphasizes hospital care.

10. In open systems the same final state can be reached by different paths and from different initial states. This property is known as equifinality. The manager's difficulties with equifinality are finding an acceptable path from A to B and finding the initial state. Ford Motor Company and General Motors operate under very different managerial styles and arrive at similar end products. Managers who seek the "one right path" from A to B are ignoring the property of equifinality.

11. A social-technical system is different from a biological open system in that the former has great capacity to rearrange its component parts quickly and to maintain its systems integrity. A biological system can rearrange or modify its parts only in a slow manner (through evolution) while continuing to maintain its systems integrity. A maximum rate of change for social-technical systems that allows the preservation of systems integrity has not been defined. Does adding a Department of Energy to the U.S. government exceed the rate of change that allows maintenance of systems integrity? Can massive product change within a corporation change the corporate system? When the systems function changes, does the system change? For example, the Coca-Cola Company decided to purchase large numbers of orange groves. Does it remain a soft-drink-producing system or is it now dominated by the management of citrus crops?

Summary

The understanding of systems is a useful analytical tool that contributes to an understanding of the organization. The organization is an open system and must be understood as such. A knowledge of various component parts of the organization can assist in diagnosing the potential causes of the organization not reaching its desired goals and can also suggest strategies for correcting organizational behavior.

The interaction of the organization with its environment is one of the most important considerations in organizational analysis. Interaction patterns between the environment and the organization create a dynamic situation that demands careful attention. Without this attention to the interaction between the environment and the organization, the changes that occur in the organization as a result of external pressure from the environment might not be understood, and an oversimplified reaction of increased rigidity can occur.

Notes

[1] Frank J. Clark, Ronald Gale, and Robert Gray, *Business Systems and Data Processing Procedures* (Englewood Cliffs, N.J.: Prentice-Hall, 1972), p. 37.

[2] Frank Baker, "Introduction: Organizations as Open Systems," in *Organizational Systems: General Systems Approaches to Complex Organizations*, ed. Frank Baker (Homewood, Ill.: Irwin, 1973), p. 8.

[3] John P. Van Gigch, *Applied General Systems Theory* (New York: Harper & Row, 1974), p. 44.

[4] Kenyon B. De Greene, *Sociotechnical Systems* (Englewood Cliffs, N.J.: Prentice-Hall, 1973), p. 33.

[5] Dan Voich, Jr., Homer J. Mottice, and William A. Schrode, *Information Systems for Operations and Management* (Cincinnati: South-Western, 1975), p. 340.

[6] De Greene, *Sociotechnical Systems*, p. 12.

[7] J. Feibleman and J. W. Friend, "The Structure and Function of Organization," in *Systems Thinking*, ed. F. E. Emery (Middlesex, England: Penguin, 1969), pp. 30–55.

[8] D. Katz and R. L. Kahn, *The Social Psychology of Organizations* (New York: Wiley, 1966).

[9] Jay W. Lorsch and Paul R. Lawrence, *Organizational Planning: Cases and Concepts* (Homewood, Ill.: Irwin, 1972), pp. 38–48.

Organizations as Complex Systems

6

Introduction

In Chapter One organizations were defined as complex social units specifically designed to achieve a desired result. The key elements in understanding organizations have been examined. The information flows and information processing functions that take place in every organization have been described. In Chapter Three the selection and distortion characteristics of information processors were considered, and the fact that organizations share these characteristics was illustrated. In Chapters Four and Five the organization was seen as a system, and the elements of systems were defined. It was noted that understanding organizations requires an understanding of open systems and how organizations behave as open systems.

Definition

At this point it is necessary to realize that organizations are not only open systems but also complex systems. Anyone who has dealt with an organization, from one as small as the neighborhood drug store to one as large as an international diversified conglomerate, would recognize the complex nature of organizations. Our instincts tell us that organizations are difficult to understand and that it is difficult to deal with all of the interrelationships that take place within the organization and between the organization and its environment. The multiplicity of inputs, process functions, output, feedback systems, and feedforward systems supports our instincts. When the complex interaction that an organization has with its environment is added to that multiplicity, then it is clear that understanding organizational behaviors is no simple task.

It is difficult to define a complex system exactly. The following is the definition that will be used in this analysis: A *complex system* is one with many subsystems, each of which has a great deal of independence, thus creating a wide variety in the pattern of interactions among subsystems and the environment and high levels of information flows across boundaries between subsystems. In complex systems there is a constant need for coordination among the subsystems. Compared with simple systems, each subsystem has greater autonomy in choosing its own behavior while attempting to meet the overall goals of the system.

A subsystem is a piece of a system that can be viewed as a system itself with its own inputs, processes, and outputs. While we are interested in the organization as a system, for analytical purposes we will break it down into subsystems. For example, while a chain of department stores may be of interest to us, we would also be interested in subsystems such as each individual store, the centralized accounting department for the entire chain, and the personnel offices. In most of today's organizations we are interested in many levels of subsystems. If we go back to our example of the department store chain, we can see a variety of subsystems that are of interest. Each level of a subsystem is a piece of the total chain and also a piece of the higher-level subsystem of which it is a part (see Figure 6-1).

A system is complex because of its need to exchange information with other unpredictable systems in the task environment. The *task environment* consists of the functions or activities that the organization (system) must perform to accomplish its goals, plus all the inputs and outputs to the system during the performance of these functions. The unpredictability of the task environment creates the need for various subsystems to have higher levels of autonomy and independence so that they can respond appropriately to the changes in the situation. Complex systems are characterized by a high number of interactions between subsystems within the system and a great degree of freedom of action for each subsystem. Therefore, the complexity of the total system is determined by the characteristics of the subsystems, their dependence vs. autonomy, which is measured by the need for information exchange between the subsystems.

An example will help clarify the point. A typical complex system can be described as a corporation that has several units that respond independently to environmental concerns. The corporation might have a personnel office, a purchasing office, a research and development division, a marketing and sales division, and a production division, each of which must respond to external environments in order to achieve corporate goals. Because the external environments that must be dealt with are unpredictable, it is necessary for the organization to grant a reasonable degree of autonomy to each of the subsystems so that they will function effectively. Therefore, the

Figure 6-1

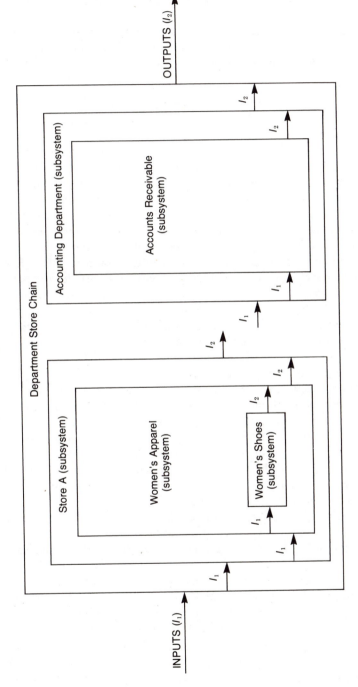

personnel division would have a great deal of freedom when dealing with a fluid labor market and when attempting to match the resources in that labor market with the needs of the organization. Similarly, the purchasing division would be granted autonomy in dealing with a variable market for raw materials so that it would best serve the total organization by providing necessary raw materials at a reasonable price.

Complexity and Size

It is possible to have an extremely large organization that is not complex. This occurs when the organization exists in a predictable task environment and when there is a minimum need for continuous interaction among subsystems. Most large automobile production plants are not complex. This is not to say that there is not a high level of technology used to perform the transformation functions; but the automobile plant does not deal with a wide variety of unpredictable environments. Through careful development of feedforward systems, the automobile plant has developed planning strategies that enable it to reasonably predict the behavior of the labor market and of the raw material market. Also, the output functions of the automobile plant are well specified in terms of corporate goals and expectations. There is a widely accepted standard operating procedure utilized to guide the functions of the workers in the production plant, which minimizes the need for information interchanges between subsystems during the production process.

Conversely, a small organization can be extremely complex if it is made up of autonomous subsystems that act with an unpredictable environment and create a need for information exchange among subsystems. An example is a neighborhood health clinic, where doctors work together for profit and community health but each doctor is also independently concerned about relationships with his or her patients. Because there is a joint effort in the health clinic to make a profit and to improve community health care, it is necessary for the doctors to communicate with each other about financial considerations and patterns of health care. This interchange normally involves a relatively extensive information flow system that is used to coordinate the activities of this complex, although small, organization.

Nevertheless, it should be noted that size and complexity are generally related, because a large organization has a much broader organizational boundary. The organizational boundary serves as an interface for the exchange of information between the organization and its environment. Inputs entering the organization from the environment pass through the organizational boundary as do outputs passing from the organization to the environment. Size is not linearly related to complexity but tends to be logarithmically related.[1] In the initial stages of an organization's growth, complexity tends to grow very rapidly; but with more established organizations, complexity does not change as rapidly as size. Ultimately, the relative independence and autonomy of the subsystems in the organization and the need for information exchange between the subsystems determine the complexity of an organization.

Evolving Complexity

In an organization, complexity is a changing characteristic. An organization might be extremely complex at one point in its development because its task environment is quite variable and because much of the information flow is nonroutine and demands an information exchange among subsystems. As the organization matures, although it may not change in size, it changes in its ability to influence its task environment and in its ability to treat the information flows within it as routine while still making a profit. It is necessary to recognize that complexity is not an either/or situation but a continuum. There are varieties of complexity within and among organizations. Some organizations are more complex than others, and one organization can be more complex at a given moment in its history than at other moments. To add to the difficulty of analysis, there is a variety of complexity within the organizational system. Within any organization some subsystems tend to be more complex than others; for example, the personnel function of a given operation might have to deal with a highly unpredictable task environment and require a higher level of information interchange, but that does not mean that all of the subsystems of the organization are complex. Within a total organization it is possible to identify subsystems that are very complex and other subsystems that are comparatively simple.

Understanding Complex Systems

To analyze organizations, they must be understood as complex systems. One of the ways to do this is to break the system down into smaller units that are easier to understand. This process, however, is not always as useful as it first appears. The synergistic property is a property of open systems, and it means that the whole is greater than or different from the sum of its parts. Because of this it can happen that a person can understand each part of a system and still be unaware of the true nature of the whole system. This will often lead to errors in analysis, such as directing an organization toward the achievement of the wrong goal. Breaking a system down into smaller parts also optimizes the behavior of subsystems but does not optimize the behavior of the total system. This occurs because the behavior of the total system is more than the behavior of the subsystem.

An example is the assembly of parts to make an automobile. The best carburetor, the best differential, the best transmission, and the best engine do not necessarily assemble into a system called an automobile. A novice, failing to understand the automobile, might choose the best elements without dealing with the interactions between them.

Another strategy for understanding complex systems is to observe critical information variables and critical information transformation functions. This is done through a process called modeling. The analyst models the system by identifying the critical information flows and the critical information processing functions and by translating this understanding into an understanding of the whole system. A critical systems element is defined as an element that, when it changes, causes a significant shift in systems characteristics. Critical systems interactions are those that determine the basic nature of systems functioning.

Identifying critical elements and interactions is extremely difficult. Without total understanding of a complex system, it is almost impossible to tell what is critical and what is not. When a model is being built because the system is too complex to be understood without it, it is easy to see why the selection of critical elements and interactions is extremely difficult. Confronted with this situation, the model builder or analyst might resort to using as critical elements those variables or information flows that are easy to measure and those interactions that are easy to model with a mathematical equation. While these techniques might lead to an elegant mathematical model, the behavior of the model can be radically different from the behavior of the system, and thus the model will make no real contribution to systems understanding.

An example of this phenomenon occurs in the construction of a mathematical model of an oil refinery. On the surface, an oil refinery is not a very complex system, because it is possible to make relatively accurate forecasts of both supply and demand, and there is a good understanding of the technological processes involved in the information transformations. Therefore, it is natural to build a mathematical model of the operation of an oil refinery and use an understanding of this model to understand the behavior of the refinery. But should the refinery workers go on strike for higher wages because of inflation, the mathematical model of the refinery operation will not work if it did not include the critical variable of increased government spending, which drives up inflation. A strike of refinery workers would completely close down the refinery and prohibit further information processing, although the model might predict that the refinery will produce a certain quantity of oil. Clearly the model would lead to an incorrect prediction because it could not capture the total complexity of the system.

These pitfalls cannot be avoided entirely because systems are complex, and the interactions within systems and between systems are exceedingly difficult to describe. An understanding of the complex nature of systems can avoid some of the more common errors, and the remainder of this chapter is devoted to a discussion of some of the factors that create complexity in the system and some of the factors that can be used to analyze organizations.

A Conceptual Model

Since complex systems are characterized by their ability to deal with relatively unpredictable environmental inputs, it is necessary to develop a conceptual model of the system that extends beyond the one developed in Chapter Four. The purpose of this model (Figure 6-2) is to help the reader understand the nature of a complex system.

Figure 6-2

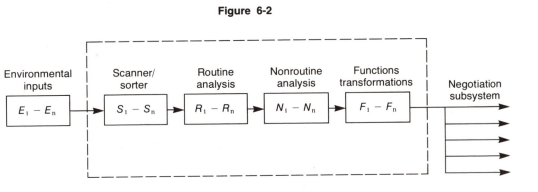

Environment   The environmental inputs E_1–E_n are the information flows from outside the system that affect the operation of the system but over which the system may have no direct control. There are, of course, information flows in the environment over which the system not only has no control but which do not affect the operation of the system.

Scanner/Sorter Subsystems   The scanner/sorters, S_1–S_n, represent subsystems that scan the environment and identify the information flows necessary for systems performance. In addition, these subsystems sort the information flows and direct them to appropriate parts of the processing function. An example of a typical scanner/sorter function in an organization is the personnel department, which scans the labor market and identifies those people who are suitable future employees for the organization. It then provides ways to bring those people into the right part of the organization by sorting them through various personnel processes. The distribution of information from the environment within the organization is not a random or capricious distribution. Rather, the various scanner/sorter functions, by dealing successfully with the environment, identify the critical information flows and direct them to the appropriate part of the system. If the environment were totally predictable, there would be no need for a scanner/sorter function because its activities could be incorporated into standard operating procedures. It is because the environment, E_1–E_n, is not predictable that the various scanner/sorter subsystems, identified as S_1–S_n, are necessary.

Scanner/sorter subsystems must prevent information overload on the total system. They do this by screening out the irrelevant and inappropriate information flows and by letting into the organization only those that are relevant. Sometimes it is necessary for the scanner/sorter to reject information that is in fact relevant simply because the system cannot tolerate additional information at a particular time. For example, the order taking and production scheduling department of an organization will occasionally reject a customer's order to keep the scheduled production within capacity. The scanner/sorter selects appropriate information from the environment to make the system work. Scanner/sorter subsystems are aware of changes in the environment that affect the information requirements of the system. In addition, scanner/sorter systems maintain a sensitivity to the needs of the system.

A personnel office that is functioning appropriately does not send too many new employees to a given unit for interviews when that unit is too busy with other projects. In evaluating the labor market, an effective personnel office can recognize changes in educational and training programs that would create a different type of applicant for jobs. The personnel office then alerts elements within the system to these changes and readjusts its sorting and screening procedures to accommodate these changes.

Additional examples of scanner/sorter systems that are found in most organizations include purchasing departments, research and development units, receptionists, and "technical gatekeepers," who monitor technical information in the environment. The purchasing department of a manufacturing firm receives information from the functional subsystem about what materials are required to meet organizational goals. The purchasing system then scans the external environment for good material at good prices and then purchases enough to maintain an adequate inventory. Thus, the scanner/sorter system interfaces with the external environment as well as with other subsystems in the system. Unfortunately, much information can be lost in the transfer of information, such as between the functional subsystem and the purchasing department or between the purchasing department and the environment. This loss of information, often due to selection and distortion properties of the scanner/sorter subsystems, reduces the effectiveness of the scanner/sorter system.

Systems that serve dual roles, such as the U.S. Army in peacetime and in war, must change the role of the scanner/sorter devices when the organization must function in a different role because of an environmental change. As a result, the scanner/sorter must change either the variables it measures or change the relevant measurement points on the same variable. An example is the condition under which a personnel office, operating in a tight labor market condition, scans and sorts, using active recruitment and intensive training of new employees. In a loose labor market, the same personnel office might scan and sort mainly to keep people out of the system because there is an overabundance of qualified, trained personnel. A purchasing office must change its measurement indices if an external supplier of a raw material joins a cartel and an embargo results. Here a price for required material, which would have been screened out of the system because it was unreasonable, is not screened out because the environment has changed significantly.

Figure 6-3 illustrates the conditions where the organization alters scanner/sorter elements to meet changes in the environment. The scanner/sorter subsystems have to respond to conflicts created by shifts and changes in the task environment.

Figure 6-3. Organizations That Must Alter Scanner/Sorter

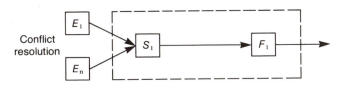

Single organizations that play dual roles, such as an insurance company that sells both personal life insurance and industrial insurance, can also have dual scanner/sorter devices. There is frequently a conflict between the two scanner/sorter devices and between the variety of functional transformation elements. For example, a hospital administrator must remember that the task in the emergency room is different from the task conducted in the rest of the hospital. Patients are admitted and treated differently in both places. Both areas may check the same variable but watch for different critical measurements, or they can monitor entirely different variables due to the difference in their roles.

Figure 6-4 illustrates the condition where the organization has dual functions and dual scanner/sorter devices. The organization has internal stress between functions F_1–F_n and scanner/sorter systems S_1–S_n. These must be resolved through internal information exchanges in order for the system to respond appropriately.

Figure 6-4. Organizations with Dual Functions and Dual Scanner/Sorter Devices

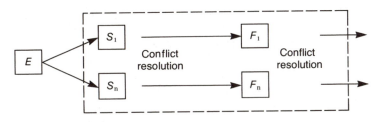

The scanner/sorter subsystems within an organization are the major way that the organization interfaces with the task environment. Under the conditions where there is a complex system, where the task environment E_1-E_n is unpredictable, it is necessary to have a variety of scanner/sorter subsystems, S_1-S_n, and these subsystems must be quite sophisticated information processors in order to serve the needs of the total organizations.

Routine Analysis Subsystems   After information is brought into the organization through a scanner/sorter subsystem, a variety of analyses must take place in order for the critical information to be rendered routine. These routine analysis subsystems, R_1-R_n, are extremely important. These are the subsystems that operate to develop the processes and procedures for the classification and categorization of routine information in the system. These subsystems often serve as key interfaces between scanner/sorter systems and transformation functions. One of their major roles is to develop a set of standards by which many decisions are made. For example, an airline steward or stewardess must be between five feet and five feet ten inches tall without shoes on. This limitation is necessary because of physical characteristics of airplanes and because of certain physical demands of the job situation. The airline must have a way to develop this set of standards and to measure the input information against these standards.

Similarly, organizations must develop a set of rules about how information gets from one point in the organization to another. These rules might include such things as reporting relationships between subsystems as well as standard operating procedures for establishing an information flow from one point to another. For example, in order to enter graduate school, a student must normally have completed 120 to 130 undergraduate semester hours of education from an accredited institution of higher education.

One of the difficulties in the development of routine information analysis subsystems R_1-R_n is that they tend to become overcommitted to one type of information flow. Basketball coaches should evaluate a player's potential using variables other than height, such as vision, endurance, and skill; it is not enough for a person to be tall enough to play basketball. Another example is the way a customer is treated in a bank—it should not be a function of physical appearance, since physical appearance can mask considerable wealth or considerable poverty. It is necessary for bank employees to be trained not to become overly dependent on physical appearance as a way of determining the appropriate treatment of a bank customer.

Not only do routine analysis subsystems tend to become overcommitted to a single measurement criterion, they also tend to become overcommitted to a particular solution set, using it regardless of the problem or the type of information flow. Managers often see every relationship as linear and fail to recognize that some relationships may be curvilinear. For example, the ratio of salespeople to sales is probably not linear. Simply adding one more salesperson does not guarantee a proportional increase in the number of sales. Other examples are the manager who becomes overcommitted to average sales and fails to deal with extremes and the manager who looks at the average sales per month for a given salesperson and fails to realize that in some months the salesperson is selling well above average and some months well below. A similar case occurs in piecework analysis on production lines. This kind of analysis looks at the average number of products produced by a worker in a week; thus, it could overlook that a worker produced all of his or her products on Monday, Tuesday, and Wednesday and nothing on Thursday and Friday. While such a worker met the average weekly production rate, there is great variance in the productivity when viewed over a shorter time frame. The point here is that routine information analysis subsystems can become overcommitted to solution sets.

Another example of misapplication of routine information analysis is the routine information subsystem that views as important those things that it can do and as unimportant those things that it cannot do. For example, personnel tests receive emphasis because they can be administered, despite the fact that they might not be good predictors of future job success. It is the fact that the test can be given and scored that makes it important, not the fact that it is closely related to the potential employee contribution to the job situation.

Nonroutine Analysis Subsystems   Organizations should understand that routine information analysis subsystems R_1-R_n are capable of dealing with limited kinds of information. If information is processed by some technique that is not valid, the results are meaningless or can be more harmful than no information at all. Managers sometimes try to force understanding of data that they do not understand and to create information out of a data flow that is not relevant information to the situations under consideration. As an example, the worth of data collected in a study of the effects of information on decision making is weakened by the inability of researchers to get managers to admit that they deal with information that they do not understand. Managers tend to feel that they must say that they understand everything that they do or else be considered inept.

It is known that much of the information processed in an organization is nonroutine; therefore, there must be nonroutine analysis subsystems, N_1-N_n. These nonroutine analysis subsystems are designed to analyze information that is not readily quantifiable and for which standards are not readily available. In the absence of standards and of the ability to quantify, it is necessary for the organization to judge the information flow, utilizing the value system of the organization to interpret the information flow.

Organizations tend to treat all information as routine or nonexistent and therefore fail to deal with critical nonroutine information flows that affect the future of the organization. Managers who have primarily worked with routine information flows and who are put into situations where much of the information is nonroutine can find it difficult to adjust. For example, managers who have worked with production organizations that involve predictable environments, well-understood raw materials, and analyzable results often find that if they attempt to move into a human service organization or into an educational organization, where the inputs are not very well understood and where processes are ill defined, they have difficulty applying their managerial and organizational skills. This is a case of a manager who is unable to utilize a nonroutine analysis subsystem to deal with a complex task environment.

There are many ways that organizations have developed successful strategies for applying judgment and values to nonroutine information flows. Organizations will appoint a widely recognized leader and then assign to that leader the task of interpreting nonroutine information. Having members of the organization elect a leader to perform the role of interpreting nonroutine information is another approach the organization may employ. Socialization processes within the organization tend to teach all of the members of the organization the appropriate responses to nonroutine information. Apprenticeships and other hiring practices involving training are also used to insure that the organization has enough employees whose values and judgment are consistent with those of other members of the organization. There are many group techniques, including task forces, team building, and appropriate uses of committees, that can be used to assure that the appropriate judgments and values are used to make analyses of nonroutine information. The goal in the analysis of nonroutine information is to fit that information into a form that can be understood by the organization. Only through this technique can the organization successfully utilize the nonroutine information in the system.

It can be seen from this discussion that organizations that deal with unpredictable environments must have a great amount of information exchange among the various subsystems. It is necessary to understand the different kinds of subsystems that exist within the organization. In particular, understanding the scanner/sorter subsystems (S_1–S_n), routine analysis subsystems (R_1–R_n), and nonroutine analysis subsystems (N_1–N_n) is required in order to comprehend the nature of the interactions.

Functional Transformation Subsystems   The functional transformations F_1–F_n in a system represent the major purposes or reasons for the existence of the system. These are the processing functions that were discussed in Chapter Four. Organizations transform information in a variety of ways to make it more useful to society. They add value to information by relocating it or changing its form. It is these functional transformations that must be accomplished in order for the organization to have relevance.

Normally the functional transformations F_1–F_n in an organization are thought of as involving its core technology. The organization is typically defined not in terms of personnel functions, purchasing functions, marketing functions, or analysis functions, but in terms of its core technology as a retail sales organization, assembly production organization, manufacturing organization, or sales organization. This core technology must be buffered from changes in the task environment by the scanner/sorter system and by the routine and nonroutine analysis systems so that it can function properly. Theoretically the people who operate the functional transformation subsystems could accomplish the functions of scanning/sorting, routine information processing, and nonroutine information analysis. However, because the environment is unpredictable, these other functions are necessary.

Negotiation Subsystems   The goals or desired output of complex systems are not set by single individuals or by stable forces. Rather, as shown in Figure 6-2, there is a negotiation system that often includes people outside as well as inside the organization. The role of the negotiation system is to determine objectives and goals for the organization. In negotiating the expected outcome of an organization, it is assumed that expected or desired outputs will lead to behavior in the subsystems that in turn leads to production of the expected outputs. It is assumed that the form of the system follows the expected function of the system. Cyert and March, in their book *A Behavioral Theory of the Firm*, talked about the notion of side payments being used in the negotiation subsystem to bring about desired changes in the expected results and the desired changes in the operation of the system.[2] For example, in order to interest an aluminum company in using scrap aluminum for the production of finished products, the plant manager might be given a bonus or additional technical assistance as a side payment. In this way the plant manager is enticed into changing his or her expected outcomes and processes in order to meet the new condition set up by the negotiating subsystem.

Systems Infrastructure

The nature of the infrastructure is a function of both the core technology and of the environment with which the system deals.[3] The organization must develop a fit between the infrastructure and the environment and a fit between the infrastructure and the core technology. Buffer systems are needed to improve the fit. Examples of buffer systems are purchasing departments (between the environment and the infrastructure) and warehouses (between the infrastructure and the core). This is shown in Figure 6-5.

The more specialized the core technology, the more elaborate the infrastructure required and the less the core is able to deal directly with the environment. A good example of this is the elaborate infrastructure built up between the surgeon (highly specialized core technology) and the patient (environment). The surgeon might not deal with the patient at all until the patient is on the operating table. Likewise, a highly technical and specialized university tends to be very buffered from the community, while a community college with a relatively unspecialized core technology can have extensive contact with the environment. An organization in transition

Figure 6-5. Organization's Core Technology, Infrastructure Technology, and Environment

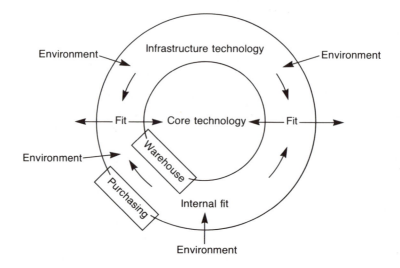

Source: Mariann Jelinek, "Technology, Organizations, and Contingency," *Academy of Management Review,* January 1977, p. 22. Reprinted by permission.

toward greater specialization can get into managerial difficulty if its infrastructures do not expand with increasing core specialization. For example, look at the firm formerly limited to production but now moving toward building a research and development division. If the personnel function (infrastructure) does not develop separate approaches for hiring in the two departments (or if two personnel offices are not opened) a serious misfit will develop. Research and development candidates can be insulted or repelled by the practices used in production hiring.

Organizations must be concerned with the management of these fits because the infrastructure itself is highly complex and has its own core technology and infrastructure. With purchasing there is a "core technology," a standard, normal, professional, expected way to get the task done. Sometimes this "infrastructure core technology" is in conflict with the basic core technology of the firm; the standard ways of purchasing are not appropriate for the basic technology of the organization. Research firms, for example, will have trouble with purchasing departments because the standard operating procedures for purchasing are basically designed for production operations.

There are multiple environmental interfaces for each core technology, so there are multiple fits required. In general, the fit between the environment and infrastructure is worse than that between the core technology and the infrastructure.

"Technological gatekeepers" (facilitators of highly technical information transfer) are a part of the infrastructure and of the core technology and must interface with both and with the environment.[4] The distances between the core technology and different parts of the environment are unequal. The industrial chemist serves as a useful example. His or her interests are related to those of an academic chemist; thus, a technological gatekeeper in this example would likely be an industrial chemist who directs information about what is going on in academia to individual industrial chemists, who might be able to use this information. Industrial chemists will also come to the technological gatekeeper when they have a problem and want to know where they should go to seek help. Yet the distance between the industrial chemist and the political environment can be vast. Here, with a great distance between the core technology and the environment, a technological gatekeeper will not work as well (see Figure 6-6).

Figure 6-6. Example of a Managerial Strategy to Deal with Complexity

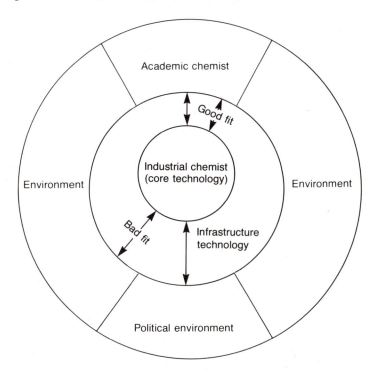

As the core technology becomes more specialized, the infrastructure must become more complex. As the core technology increases in specialization, the nature of the interactions between the core and the environment become more complex. If the organizational response is to close the system, the system becomes less effective. If it responds by building more infrastructure, it can maintain effectiveness but with a high energy cost. Organizations that skimp on administrative overhead (infrastructure) sometimes pay a price in lost efficiency and/or effectiveness that is greater than the overhead savings. There are two parts to this issue: increasing uncertainty and the need of the system for information. As the system becomes more specialized, there is a greater need for information exchange with the environment. For example, a general practitioner can deal with a great deal more uncertainty than a specialist can.

In developing a managerial strategy to deal with complexity, there are many unresolved questions. Little is known about how to design fits, and it is not known at what point infrastructure becomes dominant over the core technology. These are critical organizational issues that cannot be ignored by the analyst.

Feedback and Feedforward in Complex Systems

In addition to the elements shown in Figure 6-2, complex systems are characterized by externalized feedback and control systems that operate to control the system. There is little dependence on internal and very informal control mechanisms. Because of the fluctuation in output that might be created by fluctuations in the environment and/or misfunctions of the subsystems, it is necessary for the feedback and control loops to be carefully designed and constructed. Much of the interest in cybernetics, or self-regulating feedback and control systems, is derived from the fact that the management of complex systems involves detailed construction and analysis of the feedback system.

In addition, complex systems have externalized feedforward and planning systems. It is not adequate in the face of a complex environment for the manager simply to utilize informal simulation models that he or she creates to plan for the future of the system. It is necessary for relatively sophisticated forecasting techniques to be used and for the results of the planning function to be carefully evaluated before they are used by the system. These factors normally require highly specialized planning teams and planning subsystems that take on a character and a life of their own.

As the complexity of the organization increases, it becomes necessary to externalize the control system. With greater complexity the planning system must also be externalized. Later, a further externalized planning and control system will be added to the already externalized planning and control systems. This process is repeated as the organization grows more complex (see Figure 6-7).

As shown in Figure 6-7, control systems in complex organizations have their own feedback and feedforward loops. Because the organization is complex, control systems must be carefully planned and controlled or they will take over the organization. An inspection and quality control unit or an

Figure 6-7

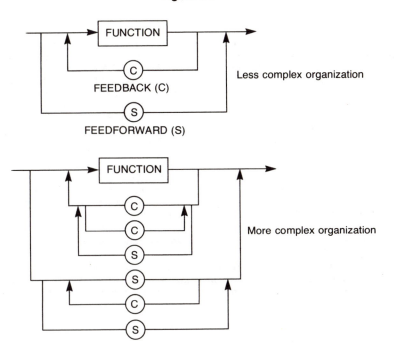

accounting control unit can come to have influence in the firm that is disproportionate to its contribution to meeting the system's goals.

Likewise, a planning function in a complex organization must have feedback control and feedforward planning, or it is likely to detract from organizational goal attainment. While planning is a positive function in most firms, it is possible to commit so many organizational resources to planning that inadequate resources are left for executing the core technology. Organizations avoid these conditions by careful management of control and planning functions.

Summary

This discussion has attempted to extend the basic systems model to include a definition of the subsystems necessary if an organization is to cope with a variable environment. The fact that the organization needs to have a variety of subsystems serving specialized functions indicates an increased need for information exchange among subsystems and for coordination among the various specialized functions. It is this variable task environment, together with the need for independence and autonomy by specialized subsystems and the need for coordination and information exchanges, that makes systems complex.

Notes

[1] Michael K. Moch, "Structure and Organizational Resource Allocation," *Administrative Science Quarterly*, 1976, *21*, 661–674. The following literature dealing with organizational size is cited by Moch: Peter M. Blau, "A Formal Theory of Differentiation in Organizations," *American Sociological Review*, 1970, *35*, 201–218; Peter M. Blau and Richard A. Schoenherr, *The Structure of Organizations* (New York: Basic Books, 1971); John Child, "Strategies of Control and Organizational Behavior," *Administrative Science Quarterly*, 1973, *18*, 1–17; D. J. Hickson, D. S. Pugh, and D. C. Pheysey, "Operatives Technology and Organization Structure: An Empirical Reappraisal," *Administrative Science Quarterly*, 1969, *14*, 378–379; D. S. Pugh, D. J. Hickson, C. R. Hinings, and C. Turner, "The Context of Organizational Structures," *Administrative Science Quarterly*, 1969, *14*, 91–124.

[2] Richard M. Cyert and James G. March, *A Behavioral Theory of the Firm* (Englewood Cliffs, N.J.: Prentice-Hall, 1963); Richard F. Vancil, "Strategy Formulation in Complex Organizations," *Sloan Management Review*, 1976, *17*, 1–18; Petro Georgious, "The Goal Paradigm and Notes Toward a Counter Paradigm," *Administrative Science Quarterly*, 1973, *18*, 291–310.

[3] Mariann Jelinek, "Technology, Organizations, and Contingency," *The Academy of Management Review*, 1977, *2*, 17–26.

[4] Thomas J. Allen, "Communications in the Research and Development Laboratory," in *Groups and Organizations: Integrated Readings in the Analysis of Social Behavior*, ed. Bernard L. Hinton and H. Joseph Reitz (Belmont, Calif.: Wadsworth, 1971), pp. 108–114.

Organizational Response to Complexity

7

Introduction

Remember that systems complexity is created by the system's need to exchange information with an unpredictable task environment. Another way of saying this is that the complexity is created by the need for system A to exchange information with an unpredictable system B. Because system A cannot predict the behavior of system B, it is necessary that system A be complex. Since the exchange of information between system A and system B creates the complexity, altering the information exchange provides techniques by which the organization can reduce the complexity. If system A finds that the interactions that are necessary between subsystems in order to deal with system B require more energy than system A desires to use, then there are strategies that it can use to reduce the complexity.

Reducing the Need for Information Exchange

The first of these strategies is to close the system or reduce the need for the information exchange. This strategy invariably reduces the probability that an organization will achieve its objectives. However, when the complexity can be reduced a great deal while the probability of goal attainment is reduced very little, the value of closing the system in order to reduce complexity can be great. The obvious and most straightforward example is when organizations utilize standard operating procedures and rules that can cause certain information to be rejected that would be useful. Because of the use of these rules, much unneeded information is rejected and system complexity is greatly reduced. Therefore, it is preferable to close the system through the use of rules.

Another general strategy is for system A to spend organizational resources to increase the ability to predict the behavior of system B. Time spent in looking at previous behavior on the part of system B or talking with members of system B about their intentions is often spent predicting the future behavior of system B and thereby reducing the complexity of system A. When developing strategies for reaching goals, the organization must weigh the relative cost of energy invested in closing the system or in improving the ability to predict system B's behavior against the energy utilized in managing organizational complexity.[1]

Buffers for Linked Systems

There are two special cases of systems complexity that are of particular interest to organizations and for which organizational strategies are often developed. The first of these is the case in which system A is linked to system B; system A does not control the behavior of system B and therefore cannot use control functions to increase the predictability of system B.

Some organizational complexity occurs because of the way in which systems elements are linked together. The manager's problem is to understand the relationships, or links, between elements and to understand why each link exists and what transactions take place at each link. Figure 7-1 represents a linked system. A look at the warehouse shows how complex the interrelationships can become. The material flowing into the warehouse is a function of the activities at the two inspection stations. As long as the flow through these points is predictable, an intake procedure can be developed that minimizes the energy expenditure at the warehouse for the predicted condition. However, the flowthrough at the inspection stations is not completely predictable. A run of bad parts or the illness of one of the inspectors can change the situation. Therefore, the intake procedure must provide enough slack to absorb such unpredictability. Likewise, the demand from the machine shops is a function of a complex set of variables in each shop. Is there a machine malfunction that creates an unusual demand condition in one of the shops? If so, how does this affect the ability of the warehouse to absorb materials from the inspection stations? Will this cause an overload at the loading dock? Will the paint shop be idle? Can workers and machines at one of the operating machine shops take up the slack? If so, will this create a different transportation path from the warehouse to the shop that takes on the extra work? The questions mount up, demonstrating the complexity created by systems linkage.

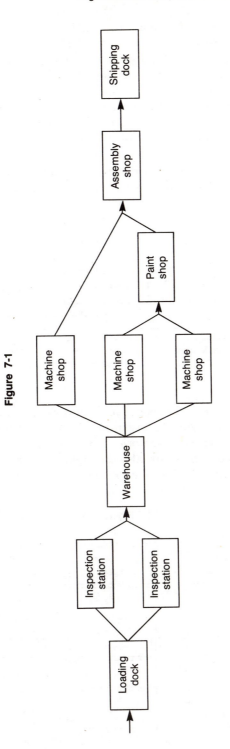

Figure 7-1

In order to relieve the complexity resulting from linkages, the organization utilizes buffers. One of the most typical buffers is a staff position. An individual occupying a staff position discharges responsibility by providing information, advice, and recommendations to line personnel; quite simply, the staff member fills the role of consultant to the line manager. Line personnel are the people who supervise and perform the primary functions of the organization in such departments as management, sales, production, and finance. The principal value of staff positions is that specialized knowledge and technology can be injected into the organization to absorb the complexity for line personnel. For example, an assistant to the president can attempt to deal with the linkage problem between vice-presidents. Figure 7-2 illustrates this relationship.

Figure 7-2

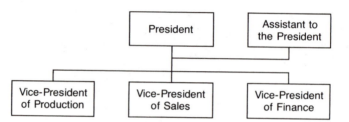

There are numerous forms of subsystems that organizations can utilize to act as buffers. Individuals, organizations, computer storages, gears and clutches in automobiles, inventories, warehouse, and space can all serve interface functions. There are also examples of human buffers with specialized knowledge and skills (see Figure 7-3). The purchasing agent uses

Figure 7-3

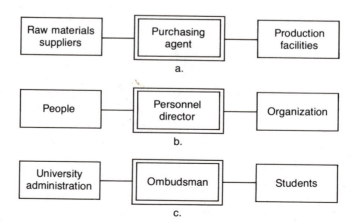

his specialized knowledge to purchase raw materials on the best terms available for the purchasing organization (in this example, the production facilities). Personnel directors of large organizations use their specialized knowledge to attract potential employees from the pools of human resources available to the organization. University administrators can structure their organization to include an ombudsman position. The ombudsman serves an interface function between the administration and the university's students.

Reorganization for Nested Systems

There is also the case where system B is a subsystem of or suprasystem to system A. In these cases there is a functional nested, or hierarchical, relationship between systems A and B. The fact that there is a hierarchical relationship leads to some additional organization strategies for dealing with complexity.

Systems often become complex when they are hierarchical. Each system derives its particular significance from the larger system of which it is a part and from the subsystems that it contains. Yet, the synergistic property of systems indicates that the larger system is greater than the sum of its parts. Figure 7-4 represents a hierarchical system.

Figure 7-4

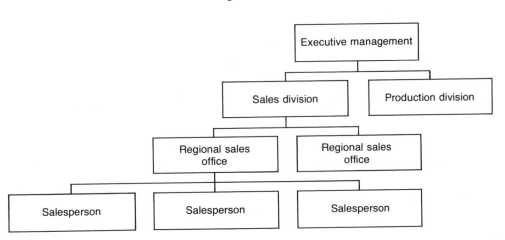

Looking at the regional sales office on the left in Figure 7-4, see how the hierarchical nature of systems contributes to complexity. The regional sales office must operate under the constraint system imposed by the sales division, and it must both compete and cooperate with the other regional sales office for attention, direction, and resources from the sales division office.

The regional sales office must develop policies and procedures to coordinate the work of the salespersons and be responsive to their particular needs. The manager of the regional office cannot act independently of the hierarchical relationships. Nor can the manager be insensitive to other hierarchical relationships in the system. For example, the regional officer might depend on the policy developed by top management to establish the salary and benefits program that can be offered to salespersons. Thus, the constraints on the regional sales office are imposed not only by the sales division but also by executive decisions. As the organization gets larger and there are more levels of hierarchy, the relationships can become increasingly complex.

All systems are hierarchical and as such have a nesting relationship with other systems. This nesting property is similar to the linkage relationships in that there are significant points of interaction. However, when thinking of nested relationships, it is necessary to be concerned with systems that are not only connected to but also integral to some other system. This creates special problems of complexity.

In order to relieve the pressure created by the nature of the hierarchical relationships, organizations rely on a reorganization scheme. This involves the rearrangement or addition of line personnel. "A relationship in which the occupant of one position can exercise direct command over the occupant of another position is called *line authority*."[2] "Anyone with complete line authority plans the activities, issues the orders, stimulates greater effort, and checks up and evaluates the performance of his subordinates."[3]

Consider the hierarchical relationships depicted for Longhorn Merchandisers, Inc., in Figure 7-5. As a result of pressure created at the store manager level of Longhorn Merchandisers, Inc., management is considering alternative organizational structures: (1) increasing the number of store managers, (2) making the store managers autonomous, (3) reorganizing the entire organization, and (4) introducing an assistant manager position. After evaluating these alternatives, management decides that its store managers

Figure 7-5. Longhorn Merchandisers, Inc.

Line Strata

Board of directors
Executive committee of the board
President
General merchandise manager
General superintendent of stores
District supervisors
Branch managers
Store superintendents
Store managers
  ➤ Assistant store manager
Clerks

will be better equipped to deal with organizational complexity if an assistant store manager position is created.

There are other reorganizational strategies for reducing complexity caused by hierarchical relationships. The development of job descriptions often reduces the uncertainty in relationships between workers and supervisors. Rules for internal budget control often make the organization less complex for subsystems because people know what is expected up and down the hierarchy in terms of budget control. Other structural changes to reduce hierarchical complexity include reports, rules, objective statements, program budgets, new line positions, and reassignments of responsibilities.

Organizations must proceed cautiously when dealing with complexity. Identification of the problem situation is extremely important. Strategies for coping with problems resulting from systems linkages are different from strategies for problems that result from hierarchical relationships.

Intrasystem Interaction

The interaction and interrelationships of subsystems within an organization contribute to complexity. One of the primary causes of intrasystem complexity is the fact that all information processors generate unanticipated outcomes that must be dealt with by the organization. One of the ways of dealing with these unanticipated outcomes is to ignore or suppress them, but often these outcomes can provide the major impetus for organizational growth and for the development of new forms. Therefore, some organizations look at these unanticipated outcomes carefully and see if these outcomes can be transformed into new information and become useful. When that strategy is adopted, a spiraling effect can occur because the new information that is generated from the unanticipated outcomes requires new information processors, and these new information processors generate additional unanticipated outcomes that can be further translated into new information.

Organizations that have both the capacity and the willingness to transform unanticipated outcomes into new information are creative organizations. The creative process is defined as manipulating unanticipated outcomes successfully from information processes so that new information is created. The transformation of these unanticipated outcomes into information is the work of creative people.

Figure 7-6 illustrates the spiraling effect and its loop nature. Creative people generate new information from unanticipated outcomes. Technology is then introduced to develop a new information processor that can be used to process that new information and to generate desired results. In addition to the desired results, unanticipated outcomes are generated, thus starting the process once again.

Different systems develop different amounts of unanticipated outcomes. Systems generating small amounts of unanticipated outcomes are less re-

Figure 7-6

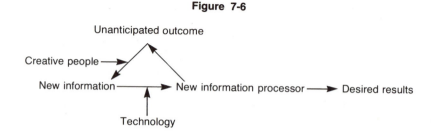

ceptive to the creative process. Thus if an organization develops a technology to process information that lessens unanticipated outcomes, the opportunities for the creative process are reduced. If organizational activities are changed to increase unanticipated outcomes through such activities as adding a research and development arm, the opportunity for creative activity is increased.

The creative process generates a phenomenon called progress. There is a spiraling effect within the organization that is continuously moved along by creative human information processors. Every attempt to deal with the complexity caused by these spiraling effects leads to increased complexity, new unanticipated outcomes, and new opportunities for the creativity process to take place. An example will illustrate this phenomenon.

During World War II, the invention of radar provided the British with information about the movement of enemy aircraft. In fact, it provided so much information that it was impossible for the existing information processes to handle the load. Therefore, the British created an operations research section to assist in processing the large amounts of information. Operations research was such a powerful information processor that it generated new information of its own, primarily mathematical strategies for analyzing systems. These strategies were used by operations researchers and others to process all kinds of information. A new subset of knowledge was created by this powerful influence, and almost all students of organizations today study operations research and are familiar with its basic concepts.

Complexity, Society, and the Individual

It will be remembered that one of the major factors of complexity in organizations was the need for information exchange among the subsystems within the organization. Looking at the nature of information in the environment helps to understand the tremendous complexity created by the need for organizations to exchange information in order to achieve their goals.

There are many different bits of information in each environment. There are symbols, objects, and physical phenomena combined in a variety of ways to provide an overabundance of information. Because of this, a person selectively perceives only a small percentage of all information available to the senses at any given moment. Take a moment and try to perceive some things you don't normally perceive. Feel your shoes on your feet or the way a chair feels on your body. Look around the room and try to notice something you don't normally see. Listen carefully and hear all of the noises that you usually ignore. Doing these things can help you understand how much information there is and how selective information processors must be in order to function.

Not only is there a large amount of information in the environment, but also these bits of information can have a large variety of relationships with each other. There are twenty-six letters in the alphabet that can be combined in countless ways to make words. These words can be combined in an infinite number of ways to construct meaningful phrases and sentences.

Not only is the amount of information in the environment staggering, but the available information processors can be combined in an almost limitless number of ways. Even a very modest camera shop can be confusing with its variety of technological information processors, such as cameras, filters, developers, and enlargers. We can get a notion of the number of different kinds of information processors in society by noting that the Dictionary of Occupational Titles lists over 15,000 different occupations in over 2,000 groups. The number of courses in a college catalogue is a modest indication of the number of collections of conceptual information processors available for study.

These numbers indicate the complexity of society. If we look at our environment at random and try to combine bits of information and choose information processors, we face an impossible task. The notion of systems helps us bring order to and produce meaning in our environment. Even so, we are left with considerable complexity within systems. There is an evolution of more complex and more sophisticated systems as the linkage, hierarchical, and spiral effects become more important in society.

Individuals pay a price for the increased progress in society. One thousand years ago the level of information processing required of the average person to survive in society was comparatively low. The environment could be dealt with by a person whose cognitive capability was minimal. Now it is very difficult for a person who cannot read to survive. Just the forms that must be filled out to qualify for unemployment compensation or welfare payments require a high degree of cognitive skills. The cognitive capacity of a person might soon be the primary limiting factor of survival; unless one has the cognitive resources to deal with a society that is becoming more complex at an exponential rate, a person might be unable to manage his or her life.

One of the primary reasons for the failure of small businesses is that they lack the information processing capacity to deal with complexity. The proprietor of a small business might be quite capable as an individual, particularly with respect to the core technology of his or her business. However, the complex set of constraints imposed by the environment can require a particular set of information processing skills that are unavailable. For example, the complexity of the legal system makes it impossible to run any kind of private business without the service of a lawyer. The proprietor of a small business can end up out of business, not because he or she is losing money, but because of failing to deal effectively with a particular set of legal information.

Summary

Organizations must deal with an unpredictable task environment and have subsystems that are autonomous and that must be coordinated through the exchange of information; thus, they must be complex. The organizational system suffers from information overload. The scanner/sorter subsystems, routine information analysis subsystems, nonroutine information analysis subsystems, and functional transformation subsystems are unable to handle the massive amount of information that must be exchanged in such a situation. If the organization is to survive, it must accommodate the information overload predicament.

In general these accommodations are made by increasing the information processing capacity of the various elements of the system.[4] This information processing capacity can be increased through the development of new technology, through the training of people in the system, and through the rearrangement of the elements of the system. Failure to adopt an organizational strategy for accommodating the uncertainties in the task environment and the needs that this creates for internal information exchange will result in the utilization of organizational slack to absorb the impact of the information pressure on the organization. For example, a company that has an exceedingly large inventory is absorbing uncertainties in the environment and uncertainties in the functional transformation processes by the maintenance of this inventory. The acquisition and maintenance of this inventory has a high cost. If the organization could develop strategies to manage the unpredictability in the task environment better and the coordination required within the organization, then the size of the inventory could be reduced and capital could be released for other uses.

There are both individual strains and organizational strains that are the result of complexity. It is only through the understanding of the complexity in the organization that the analyst can possibly assist the organization in reducing these strains.

The chapters that follow deal with specific processes and functions that take place within organizations and utilize the systems analysis developed in the first five chapters to increase understanding of organizational functioning in modern society.

Notes

[1] Frank Baker, "Introduction: Organization as Open Systems," in *Organizational Systems: General Systems Approaches to Complex Organizations*, ed. Frank Baker (Homewood, Ill.: Irwin, 1973), p. 18.

[2] Rocco Carzo, Jr., and John N. Yanouzas, *Formal Organization, A Systems Approach* (Homewood, Ill.: Irwin, 1967), p. 50.

[3] William H. Newman and James P. Logan, *Business Policies and Management*, 4th ed. (Cincinnati, Ohio: South-Western, 1959), p. 482.

[4] Jay Galbraith, *Designing Complex Organizations* (Menlo Park, Calif.: Addison-Wesley, 1973).

Organizations as Process-Following, Problem-Solving, and Decision-Making Systems

8

Introduction

The organization has been defined as a complex social unit deliberately designed for a specific purpose or set of purposes. The first seven chapters tried to increase the reader's understanding and ability to analyze organizations and thereby to develop strategies for the successful management of these organizations. Certain concepts have been developed in order to enhance this understanding.

Information has been identified as the key variable in understanding organizations. The differentiation between routine and nonroutine information is important because organizations process routine information very differently from nonroutine information. Most of the literature on organizations and management describes processes that are appropriate for routine information-processing systems. It is clear from an observation of the development of modern organizations that the amount of critical information that is nonroutine is increasing; thus, it is necessary for the analyst to understand both routine and nonroutine information and how both types are handled differently.

Different kinds of information processes—technological, conceptual, and human—have been described, as well as their types and characteristics. Selection and distortion characteristics of the information processes have been particularly emphasized because they often determine the very nature of the information processor and its capacity to assist the organization in achieving organizational goals.

The notion of organizations as systems was then explored. There is a functional relationship between the information flows and the information processors that defines a system. The elements of open systems and the characteristics of open systems have been discussed. The complex nature of organizations as systems and the interaction of the environment and systems have been emphasized. The total perspective has been that organizations are open systems with permeable boundaries that are subject to environmental pressure. The success of the organization in managing the environmental pressure while achieving organizational goals is a major concern in the analysis of the organization.

We have been attempting to describe the fundamental concepts necessary to understand the structure and management of organizations. In this chapter, the basic concepts are combined to describe organizations as process-following, problem-solving, and decision-making systems.

A significant majority of the activities occurring in organizations can be described as process following. The organization's people and machines work to accomplish its goals and objectives by using routine information and specified processes and procedures to obtain desired results. Process following uses a path of previously chosen standard operating procedures to process routine information for standard results—the organization's desired objectives.

When the organization's present output does not equal its desired output, the organization has a problem. In problem situations, organizational mechanisms attempt to modify systems operations so that the actual output is the same as the desired. When proper corrections are made in the organization's current information inputs or processes, the organization will again achieve its desired objectives. These events characterize another basic organizational process known as problem solving. Problem solving involves two distinct activities: determining when output does not equal the desired objective and finding a path or paths, which may include modifying the system.

Once one or several alternatives describing paths that can be taken are available, a decision can be made. Decision making is defined as choosing between alternatives or choosing to accept or reject a single alternative.

This chapter elaborates on the three basic organizational processes—process following, problem solving, and decision making. These managerial activities can be summarized as follows: *process following*—following a predetermined and highly specified path (set of actions) to achieve a desired objective; *problem solving*—determining when actual output does not equal desired output and then finding a path that will achieve the desired objectives; and *decision making*—choosing the path to be followed or choosing to accept or reject a single alternative.

Daily Routine

Organizations are assembled to accomplish specific sets of objectives. Today's organizations are composed of many human (individual and group) and technological information processors. Together, the two categories of information processors produce products and services that society associates with organizations.

Most people spend each day interacting with hundreds of organizations. They wake up to the morning news being broadcast on the radio station; snatch the morning edition of the newspaper off the front yard or balcony; board the bus operated by the municipal transportation department; stop at the medical clinic to set up an appointment for their annual physical; receive the morning mail from the post office; buy coffee, doughnuts, and a package of gum at the drug store; call their answering service to say "good morning" and get morning messages using the telephone system—and the day has just begun.

Standard Operating Procedures

Each of the organizations mentioned in the preceding paragraph behaves in a predictable, recognizable, and standard fashion. Consequently, interactions with these organizations are routine. Most individuals generally follow the same pattern each working day of the week. Services and products provided by these organizations are the output of their information processors performing their standard operating procedures to obtain their standard results.[1]

To reiterate, the majority of individual interactions with hundreds of organizations is very predictable because the operations of each organization are themselves routine. For example, consider the law firm of Smith, Jones, and Brown, which is typical of many small service organizations. It consists of three partners, Jim Smith, Elizabeth Jones, and Sam Brown; two new law associates, Bob Adams and Ann Fredericks; an office administrator, Judy Ward; and two secretaries, Linda Gonzales and Bill Rogers. As with many small businesses, the general atmosphere is informal. There are frequent friendly gestures among the eight people in the office; it is clear that all consider the office a nice place to work. Observing the interactions that take place reveals that the firm is well organized and operates smoothly. A large proportion of the activities of the office are routine, even though the activities of each employee are diversified.

The two secretaries spend most of their time typing and responding to inquiries from clients and outside attorneys. Judy, as office administrator, spends time handling the records. Her duties include preparing bills to clients, paying office expenses and bills, and crediting client payments as they are received. The functions that Linda and Bill perform consist of a well-defined set of secretarial routines; they transform dictated and handwritten material into finished legal documents and letters. Usually they receive dictated notes that also include detailed instructions; for example, if a client requests a new will, one of the secretaries is instructed to go to the file on wills. The secretary then prepares the new will document by copying verbatim the respective paragraphs in the will file and then inserting the client's name, address, and beneficiaries to complete the document.

Linda's function as a receptionist is also routine. She answers the phone in the same fashion each time it rings: "Hello, Smith, Jones, and Brown, law offices." She has been given a procedure to follow when the caller asks to speak with one of the attorneys: She says, "I'll see if the attorney is in and available." If the attorney does not take the call, she records the telephone call on the office log, which indicates whom the call was for, the date, the time, who called, and any message the caller wanted conveyed. Linda also is responsible for opening and distributing the mail. If the envelope is addressed to one of the attorneys, it is put on his or her desk. If a piece of mail pertains to general firm business, she deposits it on Jim Smith's desk; if a piece of mail includes a check or invoice, Linda deposits it on Judy Ward's desk.

Judy uses a routine in each of her jobs. Checks and invoices are put in her accounting in box. At the end of the week, she takes her accounting in box, determines which client the payment should be credited to, and enters the amount in a book of clients' accounts. To process an invoice, Judy writes a check and attaches the invoice. She then places it on Jim Smith's desk. Jim signs all the checks.

The law associates also perform many routine activities. Generally, Ann Fredericks handles the firm's divorce cases. When a client comes in with a domestic problem, Ann first performs the expected social amenities. Then, using a form that has a list of questions that she asks the client, she obtains information relevant to the divorce action and writes the client's responses on the form. This information includes the spouse's name and occupation, reasons for incompatibility, date of marriage, names of children (if any), joint assets, and so on. Once Ann gets the desired information from the client, she initiates a routine consisting of a prescribed series of steps that are to be taken by herself, her secretary Bill, and the client.

Looking at the office operations and the functions performed by each individual, we see that most tasks are routine. The inputs are perfectly understood and standard operating procedures are used to respond to the routine inputs. These routine activities are evident at subsystems levels, such as Judy mailing all outgoing mail when she leaves at 5:00 p.m., as well as at the overall systems level, such as the normal working schedule for the eight people in the firm. If one of the secretaries is unavailable for part of the day, Judy is notified. Attorneys use the dictating machines on their desks to compose letters and memoranda. At the end of a tape or at any time that an attorney needs a tape transcribed, he or she takes it to Judy or leaves it on her desk, and Judy then gives it to one of the secretaries or transcribes it herself if she is not busy. Letters are typed on the firm's letterhead using a standard format so that all Smith, Jones, and Brown letters are consistent. A copy of each letter is made for the firm's client files.

Because there are so many routine processes—literally thousands—in the law office, it is impossible to describe all of them. But it is important to recognize that numerous routines have been developed, which together represent the major activity of the law firm. To outsiders, the law firm's operations may look nonroutine and nonunderstandable. To the eight employees, their jobs consist of a diverse array of standard operating procedures that they perform each day. The information they receive in their jobs is routine, they understand it, and they know exactly what standard operating procedures they are to follow.

Organizational Selection and Distortion

The supermarket is familiar to everyone. Every person knows exactly where to find dairy products, vegetables, cereals, canned fruit, and coffee. Regularly patronizing a store, a person learns the location of its express lane, the day of the week that the store receives fresh vegetables and meat, the day it has special sales, and hundreds of other standard operating procedures. Most of the supermarket's operations are routine. It receives deliveries at specified times each day from company warehouses and local distributors. For example, the bread distributor might come to the store every morning at approximately 8:30 a.m. and stock the appropriate shelves with fresh bread and remove the older bread. Likewise, the behavior of checkout clerks, stock persons, and managers incorporates routine information and standard operating procedures established by the food chain's central office.

The supermarket's standard operating procedures result in selection and distortion. Hundreds of examples can be cited to illustrate the supermarket's selection mechanisms. For instance, the store stocks thousands of items, which represent only a small percentage of the food, beverage, cosmetic, and drug items that are available. The store's standard operating procedures determine which items will be carried. The movement of low-volume items, such as specialty food items, are governed by a store rule requiring that the item sell in a certain quantity per month or be discontinued. In all probability, a person who enters the store to purchase a low-volume, specialty import will not find it, regardless of the product's quality or desirability.

There are other rules. The supermarket carries only national brands that are available to all stores that belong to the food chain. Accordingly, a high-quality, local product distributed in another community will not be carried by this supermarket, regardless of local demand. The store also has standard operating procedures that specify the products that it will not carry and the businesses it will not enter. For instance, it does not stock garden tools, clothing, legal services, iron ore, and heavy construction equipment, regardless of the community's need, because of store policy. The supermarket also has standard procedures that ban products with a shelf life of less than seven days. The store does not carry goods baked without preservatives, which have a shelf life of less than three days.

Standard operating procedures lead to distortion. When stocked, products are stamped with a price and are not restamped when there is a price change. Therefore, an individual will occasionally find two identical products with different prices. Similarly, the standard operating procedures used to place fruit and vegetables on the counters result in some fruit being bruised and some vegetables becoming overexposed. Distortion occurs because the routine procedures followed to stock the shelves result in small tears in packages, dented cans, and illegibly stamped prices.

The individual employees are also information processors who create distortion in the supermarket's operations. Distortion occurs when the clerk at the cash register misreads a price and rings up the wrong amount on the register or when the store manager tours the store and notices shelf problems—cans and boxes not aligned properly and products in the wrong locations—but overlooks dirt on the floor, which is contrary to the store's standard operating procedure that prescribes clean floors.

The store's routines that generate these selection and distortion effects also provide the reasons people choose to shop there: The cashiers call out each price as they register each item; any merchandise that is spoiled can be returned for a refund or an exchange; there is an express lane that is always open for six or fewer items; personal checks for the amount of the purchase plus $10 are accepted; and the store always carries low priced private labels for all high-volume canned goods.

Total Systems Operations

The last two sections have illustrated that standard operating procedures form the basis of most activities in organizations and are a key to the selection and distortion of information processed by the organization. All operations can be represented by standard operating procedures and interactions between information processors. It is important to recognize that organizations are composed of a large number of standard operating procedures.

Discussion of total systems operations will focus again on the supermarket. The operation of a large- or medium-size modern supermarket consists of thousands of standard operating procedures. It is obviously impossible to elaborate on all of them. But it can be shown how these procedures can be put together in classes to better understand the store's operation. The store has many subsystems, consisting of inputs, information processors, outputs, and feedback and feedforward mechanisms, to perform the functions necessary for a supermarket. For instance, there are subsystems to provide for the movement of food items through the store, the movement of employees performing their tasks, and the movement of customers selecting their purchases, as well as to provide store maintenance, newspaper advertising, cash movement, accounting information, maintenance of store inventory, store security, and other functions. One subsystem—the movement of food into, through, and out of the supermarket—will illustrate systems operations.

Input variables, processing activities outputs, and feedback and feedforward mechanisms of a supermarket's food movement subsystem can be seen in Figure 8-1. For each one of the information processors identified in Figure 8-1, there are hundreds of standard operating procedures, including procedures to be followed at the unloading dock when food items arrive, procedures to determine when and how the food is to be unloaded, procedures to designate when and where each category of items is to be stored, and so on.

Next, each food item is marked and put in stock. Hundreds of standard operating procedures are used to accomplish these two tasks, specifying the time of day the store is to be stocked, where prices are to be marked on each product, the prices of the products, where the products are to be placed, the amount of shelf space for each product category, and the amount of shelf space allocated to each brand and size. Output results when store personnel or customers specify that merchandise is spoiled and it is removed as trash. Output also occurs after customers check out merchandise that they have selected. The checkout process itself is composed of hundreds of standard operating procedures. Final desired output occurs when customers take the purchased items from the supermarket.

The supermarket's food movement has a formal negative feedback loop. Feedback starts with the inventory tally, which is taken once each week. The tally itself is then combined with the store's reorder list, which is based on historical food movements and marketing inputs. Historical food movements are determined by analyzing old inventory tallies. These tallies provide data about the supply of products being stocked by the supermarket—those in short supply and those that are overstocked. Marketing inputs are standard operating procedures covering quantities that should be ordered for advertised specials. The store's reorder list provides the information that determines the food items to be shipped routinely from the company warehouse. The standard operating procedures of the feedback loop result in adjustments in the store's controllable inputs (that is, merchandise shipped), which keeps the desired food items in the store and on the shelves.

The planning facility of the central office of the store chain analyzes the food movements into, within, and out of the store, the standard operating procedures of employees, and aspects of store maintenance, such as issues relating to the modification or improvement of store operations.

Only the food's movement through the store has been outlined. The supermarket's operations require that food movement subsystems constantly interact with marketing, inventory, cash movement, and transportation. Thus, consideration of the supermarket's operations requires the acknowledgement of other important subsystems. Detailed descriptions of these subsystems are kept in the written standard operating procedures and in the minds of the employees.

Figure 8-1. Supermarket Food Movement System

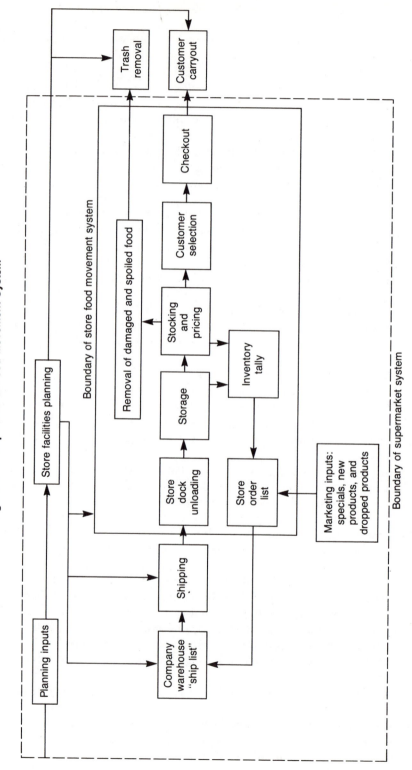

Standard operating procedures are at the heart of every organization. Studying them in great detail develops a description of the organization as a total operating system.

Organizational Slack

Organizational slack represents the excess resources in the organization that could be used to maintain existing performance, to increase output, or for problem-solving and decision-making activities. The concept of organizational slack was proposed by March and Simon in 1958 and has been used by others in describing the activities of organizations.[2] To use the law firm example once again, many of the routine activities performed by the firm's members do not necessarily support organizational objectives, although they did, in fact, support individual or group objectives. Consider, for instance, the daily practice of coffee preparation and consumption, the occasional one-and-one-half-hour lunches, and the friendly social interaction among organization members. Such slack, defined as activity that to some degree takes away from production, is found in every organization. It represents resources that could be used to increase production, solve problems, and make decisions. An organization totally without slack, however, would probably not be an attractive place to work. Furthermore, it would not have the excess capacity needed to handle nonroutine problems.

Most employees devote their time at work to process following. Employees at the lowest levels in the organization—the hourly workers—perform more activities that involve routine information processing than employees at higher levels in the hierarchy. Those at higher levels—the managers—spend a greater percentage of their time in problem identification, problem solving, and decision making.

Problem Solving

Problem management is one of the major tasks of the organization. It is best accomplished through an understanding of the system that the organization uses and of the complexity of the internal and external environment. The organization's problem becomes apparent when one of the information processors detects a current situation that is not equal to the desired objective.

In addition to formal feedback loops, there are informal feedback loops that can be used in problem identification. For example, returned merchandise to a retail sales outlet can constitute informal feedback, as can a steady loss of customers. Conversations with employees, angry customers, and even competitors can provide information that can be used to alert the store managers to the existence of a problem.

To ensure its continued survival, the organization must develop and monitor the formal feedback loops that have been designed to provide information about the most likely problem areas and the most critical problem areas. At the same time, the organization must be aware of and sensitive to information in informal feedback loops that can alert management to problem situations.

Selection and distortion created by the organization's standard operating procedures usually determine which situations are recognized as problems. This occurs in the following fashion: Management develops standard operating procedures for processing routine information. Those situations recognized as problems from information provided by formal feedback loops are usually standard problems, which can be solved through the application of standard operating procedures. While the organization's standard operating procedures are selecting routine information from the environment for processing, they are also ignoring nonroutine information from informal feedback. As a result, certain problems are likely to arise.

The key to understanding mechanisms for identifying problem situations is the organization's utilization of standard operating procedures, through which the organization specifies what is to be perceived as a structured problem situation. As a result, the organization usually develops relevant, routine solutions.

Problem recognition—based on either routine or nonroutine information—is generally considered to be a process conducted by individuals or groups. The increasing use of sophisticated automation, however, indicates that technological information processors are also capable of problem identification. Computers and other complex electronic devices are able to recognize that actual output does not equal desired output. It is generally acknowledged that only individuals or groups are presently able to process informal feedback and to identify unstructured problems.

Having determined that actual output is not equal to desired output, a system begins to work through a series of five general problem-solving steps. The steps are usually but not always sequential. The five general steps are: (1) repeating the previous activity, (2) trying an old solution, (3) trying a class of solutions, (4) trying a generalized solution, and (5) applying general systems theory. Most problems identified with normal feedback can be solved using the first three steps.

Problem Solving with Routine Information

Once a problem is found, what does the organization do? Most information processors, whether human or technological, go through a sequence of behaviors that attempt to find a path from the present situation to the desired objective. The solution is not likely to be the optimal solution unless the problem has only one solution; but given the property of equifinality for open systems (when the same desired state in a system can be reached by different paths and from different initial states), it is not logical to assume that only one solution for a problem exists. It might be assumed that it would be desirable to search for all of the possible problem solutions and then choose the one that most benefits the functioning of the system. This is not, however, what people usually do. They search for problem solutions until they find one or perhaps a few that are acceptable and then stop the search.

The first step in the problem-solving sequence is to repeat the previous activity to see if it will work on the second try. Managers often say to workers who are not performing their tasks correctly, "Let me explain this to you again." If a car does not start the first time, the tendency is to repeat the normal routine for starting it. But there is a difference in the way that the activity is done when it is repeated; most people are much more attentive to each step in the process and try to make sure that nothing is omitted and that each step is done correctly.

When repetition of the activity sequence does not solve the problem, the manager begins to examine the problem itself and asks, "Is this problem the same as or very similar to some previous problem that I have had and solved?" If the answer is yes, then the manager looks into the files of previous solutions to find the appropriate one. Once the old solution is recalled, it is applied to the existing problem. If the analysis has been correct, that is, the new problem is the same as or very similar to the old, then it is likely that this strategy will provide a solution. In fact, if a certain problem is encountered repeatedly by an organization member—for example, a manager, engineer, assembly-line worker, or personnel officer—then that organization member is likely to develop a standard problem solution for that problem.

Sometimes, however, even though the new problem looks the same as an old problem, it is not; then applying an old solution does not solve the new problem. Sometimes the new problem is obviously unlike any previous problem and there is no existing solution to try. In either case, the manager goes on to the next step in the problem-solving sequence and asks, "Is there a class of problems into which this problem fits?" The manager must call on accumulated knowledge of the various classes of problems encountered by the organization or by other similar organizations and then try to fit the problem into one of these classes. For example, the manager might ask, "Is this an accounting problem, a marketing problem, or a production problem?" If the problem can be classified, then the problem-solving techniques appropriate to that class can be implemented. Because many problems reach this stage before a satisfactory solution is found, it is very important to be aware of the different problem classes that are likely to be encountered as well as of the basic techniques for problem solving in each class. This categorization is so important to some organizations that they organize by problem classes.

Consider the familiar organization chart presented in Figure 2-1 and Figure 4-8. Each of the subsystems represented is, of course, a functional unit processing different kinds of information. Furthermore, each processor has its own information selection and distortion characteristics, and each is useful for solving certain classes of problems. A primary function that needs to be performed in an organization is the distribution of problems to the correct information processors and the consequent coordination of solutions.

Occasionally a problem will be identified by routine feedback that does not respond to the initial three problem steps. Individuals or groups within the organization are forced to resort to either a generalized solution strategy or, in very rare instances, to a general systems theory solution. At times a problem is so new and so different that the manager cannot classify it. Then the manager is forced to use a generalized problem-solving technique. Scientific method—taught in many schools—is one of the generalized problem-solving techniques that is sometimes used within organizations. Another generalized problem solution is to guess at a possible solution and then proceed by trial and error to search for a workable solution. A third generalized problem solution is to ask a superior for advice.

General systems theory is the fifth approach available:

> General systems theory, providing laws of similar structure for different fields, makes possible the use of simpler or better known models in more complicated or less controllable situations. . . . Certain general principles apply to systems, irrespective of their nature. . . .
>
> General systems theory emphasizes that there are models, principles, and laws that apply irrespective of the particular kind of system, the nature of the elements, and relations among the elements. For example, the exponential law of growth . . . applies to certain bacterial cells, to populations of bacteria, to populations of animals and people, and to numbers of publications in science, even though both the entities and causal mechanisms are different. A similar condition obtains with regard to conflict among plants, animals or nations. The mathematical laws are the same, and the entities can be considered to be systems.[3]

The "experience curve" is one example of a general systems theory solution that has achieved some popularity in the business community. The theory, popularized by the Boston Consulting Group, argues that the profitability of an organization is based on its position on the experience curve. " 'Experience curve' theory tells us that costs (exclusive of inflation) decline as volume rises, and that price also declines."[4] An organization that finds that its actual level of profits has gone down might attempt to apply the first four problem-solving procedures. If no solution is found, the organization might turn to general systems theory. The experience curve can help the organization to view its share of the market relative to its competitors' market shares. Based on this comparison, the organization could either move to acquire a larger share of the market, realizing economies as a result of larger volume, or it could leave the market. A *Business Week* article states that "the experience curve derives from the well-known learning curve theory, the time needed to perform a task decreases by a constant percentage the more often it is done."[5]

To reiterate the five steps used to achieve a desired situation, they are: (1) repeating the previous activity, (2) trying an old solution, (3) trying a class of solutions, (4) trying a generalized solution, and (5) applying general systems theory. These are essentially the standard operating procedures used by managers to solve problems. There are some limitations and pitfalls that can hinder any standard operating procedure. First, the information in the feedback loop might be incorrect. For example, based on the information in the feedback loop, a manager might think a problem results from a "worker malfunction," when actually the problem is mechanical. In such a case, the manager is blocked from finding a problem solution until the error caused by the misinterpretation of information in the feedback loop is recognized.

Second, while the information about a problem is correct, it may not help to find a solution. The thermometer indicates that the room is too warm, but it does not give the information needed to fix the air conditioner. Information in the feedback loop might point out the need to gather more information rather than indicate the appropriate strategy for achieving the desired objective.

Third, while information in the feedback loop might be appropriate, information processors involved in the system can be selecting and distorting the information in a way that blocks the discovery of a problem solution. If top management gives the same information about a problem situation to the accounting department, the marketing department, and the production department, it is highly probable that management will receive three different solutions. This occurs because each subsystem processes only selected bits of information and in specialized ways. Thus, each functional group sees a different problem and develops a different solution.

A fourth limitation on problem-identifying and problem-solving capacities of most organizations is that the collection of information needed to find and solve the problem can be extremely expensive. The cost of a quality control system can push the price of an item up so high that it becomes uncompetitive with similar products. The potential cost of undiscovered problems must be compared with the cost of installing feedback systems to discover the problems.

One of the major concerns in organizations is the tendency to become overcommitted to successful problem solutions. In fact, society often develops organizations to institutionalize a successful group of problem solutions. Then, because yesterday's solution worked on yesterday's problem, yesterday's solution is tried on today's problem. However, new problems cannot always be solved in this manner. In fact, the magnitude of the problem might be increased.

Business's fascination with computers serves as an interesting illustration of society's overcommitment to successful problem solutions. As accounts of highly successful computer applications were publicized, more and more businessmen decided that their firms' information problems and inefficiencies could be solved by getting a computer. Scores of computer companies were organized to market "canned" computer solutions for eager buyers. In some instances, businessmen were disappointed if they were informed by reputable analysts that their companies did not need computers. Many organizations were told that they needed improvements or modifications in their accounting or financial systems before computer systems could be successfully implemented. In spite of advice to the contrary, some firms did purchase computers and consequently found a significant increase in the number of reports being generated but no improvement in their problem solving. Masses of newly generated data made the search process even more complex.

Some merger and acquisition strategies exemplify classic overcommitment to structured problem solutions. Consider the case of the firm that has grown through mergers. After each takeover, management institutes massive cost cuts with employee layoffs and budget reductions, a strategy that worked for several mergers. Suddenly in one merger the organization finds that this strategy results in a severe deterioration of sales and profits. The organization has attempted to implement an old solution without recognizing that its newest acquisition had marketing or product problems rather than a cost problem.

Problem Solving with Nonroutine Information

Chapter One stated that nonroutine information is characterized by a lack of pattern, a high degree of uncertainty, and a low level of managerial familiarity. Nonroutine information can be classified as either continuous or discontinuous; the latter is characterized by irregular bursts of data. Unstructured problems are identified with nonroutine information flows and require a special set of managerial strategies if satisfactory solutions are to be found.

The manager must scan information in feedback loops to determine if it is routine or nonroutine. Often, information about problems is found in informal feedback loops. Therefore, it is particularly useful to look at this information carefully to see if it might be nonroutine.

Nonroutine information in informal feedback loops often must be transmitted repeatedly by the sender before it is received by the organization. When the nonroutine information is received, the frequent issue is to determine exactly what the problem is. It should be noted that in many nonroutine information situations, the actual definition of the problem can be as important as the procedure taken. With nonroutine information the individual or group might go through a variety of steps to define the nature and cause of an organizational problem. Frequently, unstructured situations require what only individuals and groups can provide—a creative problem-solving approach.

The unique qualities and abilities of the organization's human information processors represent excess resources, that is, organizational slack, that can be used for processing nonroutine flows of information. Most employees bring to the organization a wider range of skills than are needed to perform routine daily activities. Applying these skills and additional knowledge can be extremely important in arriving at solutions to problems. Interactions between employees that occur outside the organization, for example, contacts through mutual personal interests, contribute to the development of informal networks within the organization that can be called on to bring together nonroutine flows of information, to ask unobvious questions that help define the exact nature of an unstructured problem, and to generate alternative solutions.

If information about a problem is not like information that has been processed about apparently similar problems, then the problem probably cannot be solved with standard operating procedures. If the information does not fit into any pattern or if it is hard to organize into a meaningful structure, then the problem is likely to require different solution strategies. If the information in the feedback loop keeps coming after the solution has been implemented, the manager must attempt a nonstandard solution.

When faced with a problem indicated by nonroutine information, the manager must discover how to break the problem set. The manager must be able to discard ineffective standard operating procedures in order to see new relationships between problem elements, which in turn will lead to increased understanding. Because the problem situation is unstructured, it is difficult to suggest a sequence of activities for the manager to follow. There are, however, approaches that are used by managers to deal with such problems.

A problem can be taken to a new environment where the manager is more likely to see a possible solution. This can be as simple as leaving the office to walk around the plant while thinking about the situation. Or it can mean a management retreat, where all members of the management team leave the home office and go to a secluded area to work on problems facing the organization.

Organizations faced with problems that are characterized by nonroutine information flows often hire a new information processor, because what is nonroutine to one information processor may be routine to another. In this way, the system is elaborated. Sometimes these new information processors are hired on a temporary basis and are called consultants. Consultants often have the advantage of being able to look at problems from a new perspective and to help others in the organization look at problems in new ways.

From time to time, organizations create totally new systems to focus on problem solving. Research and development groups of most large companies are charged with the responsibility of dealing with difficult problems. Operations research had its beginnings in efforts to deal with special kinds of problems.

Experts in group dynamics have suggested strategies for using groups to solve problems. Brainstorming has gained popularity among managers as a technique for generating new ideas. During brainstorming, group members propose ideas that may help solve problem situations without judging any of the proposals. The technique generates ideas and, through group interaction, builds on them, regardless of how wild or unrealistic they might appear at first. The objective of brainstorming is to develop a totally new view or approach to a problem by letting the group be totally free to propose and discuss possibilities.

Having recognized the existence of nonroutine information in the problem environment, the manager can withhold judgment and not lock into a specific solution set. This is not done out of fear of making an incorrect assessment of the situation. Often a new idea or perspective will occur to someone else in the organization that might lead the manager to a solution that he or she would not have developed. In this way, the manager uses the informal organization. The informal organization supplements and modifies the formal structure by supporting ongoing operations and contributing to increases in organizational output, problem solving, and decision making.

Strategies that discover solutions to unstructured problems all have one thing in common: They are expensive. Because the solution effort requires behaviors that are not a part of the organization's standard operating procedures, there is likely to be a high expenditure of resources before reaching even a minimally satisfactory problem solution.

Problem Avoidance

Quite apart from problem solving, the organization is responsible for avoiding situations that pose potential problems. Problem avoidance requires the use of organizational feedforward loops that plan the organization's future (see Figure 8-2).

Planning consists of setting objectives, forecasting future conditions, and developing a proposed course of action and policies required to attain desired objectives in the light of forecasts. Planning includes comprehensive forecasting of future environmental conditions that will affect the organization. Examples of environmental components include politics, government, society, physical environment, international relations and technology (see Figure 8-3). Steiner and Miner state that

Planning enables a company to simulate the future on paper. If it does not like what it sees, it erases and starts over. This is much less expensive than letting the future evolve on an *ad hoc* basis. It applies the systems approach. It looks at a company as a system composed of many subsystems. Looking at the company in this way prevents suboptimization of parts. It forces a company to set objectives and clarifies future opportunities and threats.[6]

Figure 8-2

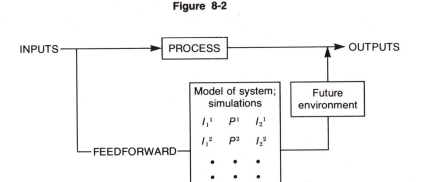

Figure 8-3.   Examples of Environmental Components

Environmental Components	Specific Issues
Politics	Party platforms
Government	Agency regulations, restrictions, and edicts
Society	Abortion and antiabortion movements
Physical environment	Offshore drilling and strip mining
International relations	Russian wheat deal and improvement of Sino-American relations
Technology	NASA's earth resources satellite

After probable future events and conditions that might affect the organization are identified, feedforward loops formulate appropriate organizational responses. These responses become the organization's short- and long-term objectives. At this time, the management of the organization sets policies—including tolerance for deviation—for the plan's implementation. The objectives specify desired systems outputs. Having identified the desired outputs, management forecasts the appropriate mix of inputs (raw materials, labor, and capital) and processes (production facilities, people, and standards) to achieve the desired objectives.

The ultimate test for effectiveness and efficiency of feedforward mechanisms is the actual results of the system. Consider the following four situations. The first two examples illustrate successful efforts to analyze the environment, while the next two demonstrate the effects of monitoring the environment incorrectly.

1.   In August 1974, Mobil Oil Company acquired Marcor, a firm that owns Montgomery Ward. The move by Mobil to diversify out of oil puzzled many

observers, since Mobil's 1973 profits increased over 1972 profits. However, despite higher profitability of oil in 1973, there was a dim forecast for the future. First, the new pricing structure of oil by the Organization of Petroleum Exporting Countries (OPEC) was expected to dissipate profits from international operations. Second, the firm correctly anticipated the end of the oil depletion allowance in the United States, thereby decreasing domestic returns. Finally, the firm was expecting the imposition of "windfall profits" taxes and other significant political pressures at home. While these last events have not yet materialized, it nevertheless seems reasonable to expect continued attempts to diminish the profits of oil companies by Congress.[7]

2.   "Back in 1968," said Hubert Clark, president of Baker Oil Tools, "we forecast an upturn in domestic drilling. It seemed to us that for balance of payments reasons it would have to go up." Having analyzed a critical element that would affect the future environment of his firm, Mr. Baker looked for and found related fields for his firm. This was a move that proved to be correct: 1974 sales were $262 million, four times higher than in 1968. This is an excellent example of correctly collecting and analyzing data from the environment.[8]

3.   In late 1973 OPEC profoundly altered the economy of the worldwide petroleum market. Shortly afterwards, a number of shipping companies and very wealthy individuals booked orders for huge new supertankers, expecting unprecedented profits from such ventures. However, by late 1974 there was an overabundance of worldwide tanker capacity, and many of these firms and individuals were forced to cancel their recently placed orders, often at a considerable financial loss. There are two primary reasons why the attractiveness of supertankers changed so drastically, both of which would have been revealed by a very careful examination of the forces that shape the profitability of supertankers. First, the increased price of OPEC oil forced consuming nations to undertake conservation efforts that would reduce their purchases; this resulted in a decrease in demand for supertanker capacity. Second, the reopening of the Suez Canal permitted tankers to navigate the canal to make the trip between Middle East refineries and Europe in twelve fewer days than it takes to sail around Africa. However, the larger supertankers cannot navigate the canal and thus are at another disadvantage. Thus, some analysts collected and evaluated the available information incorrectly, and considerable losses resulted.[9]

4.   Throughout the early 1970s, the chairman of Chrysler Corporation, President Lynn Townsend, refused to put a small car into production that would compete with the Ford Pinto and Chevrolet Vega. In 1973, Chrysler restyled its big cars at a cost of $350 million. At the beginning of the 1974 model year, Chrysler Corporation's line of compact cars was seven years old and simply not competitive with lines offered by Ford and General Motors. As the fuel crisis appeared and deepened, Chrysler sales were devastated by the lack of suitable small cars. The failure of Chrysler to analyze and act on information from the competitive sector of its environment has very nearly ruined the firm.[10]

Problem Solvers

Most organizations are designed to solve problems with routine information. Production plants, franchise operations, and schools are designed to find solutions to particular, limited kinds of problems that fit into a patterned relationship. "Future shock" that results from the continual introduction of new technology is, from one perspective, an avalanche of nonroutine information that will require new kinds of systems and new kinds of information processors for solving problems.

The closer an employee is to the top of the organization's hierarchy, the more that employee's problems tend to be characterized by nonroutine information. Employees at lower levels in the hierarchy tend to work more with problems characterized by routine information. This implies that managers have an increasing concern for the nonroutine as they move up in the hierarchy. Problem-solving skills useful and profitable at lower levels are not the same as those that are useful at higher levels. Yet employees often get promoted because of their ability to solve problems. Much of the time, the promotion is based on the employee's ability to solve the wrong kind of problem, thereby leading to a mismatch between the employee and the job. When this happens, the newly promoted person often performs incompetently. This phenomenon has been popularized by Laurence J. Peter and Raymond Hull and called the "Peter principle."[11] This problem is the responsibility of the organization, which must select individuals with the required skills or provide the necessary training for promoted employees.

Most people in organizations are process followers, not problem solvers. Process followers use standard information and follow standard routines to get standard results. This implies that the basic managerial function of process following requires following the path of selected standard processes that employ routine information to obtain standard results. The standard results are, in fact, the desired objectives.

Problem solvers, however, look at special information—*feedback*. They determine when the present situation is not equal to the desired objective; when such a condition is discovered, they look for new routines to discover the path from the present situation to the desired objective. Problem solvers are looking for new results by applying special skills and insights to structured and unstructured problem situations.

Decision Making

Managers are distinguished from other employees in the organization by the fact that they are often called on to make decisions affecting the future of the organization. Yet little is known about the variety of strategies and tactics that are used to perform this important task. Part of the difficulty is that the very definition of decision making is unclear. Often decision making and problem solving are confused, with the result that inappropriate strategies for dealing with a given situation are used. Decision making is defined as choosing between alternatives, or accepting or rejecting a single alternative. Problem solving is finding a path or paths, while decision making is choosing among paths.

When engaged in problem solving, managers find themselves confronted with alternatives and the need for decision making. While engaged in decision making, managers might discover one or more problems that must be solved. However, the information processing skills needed for problem solving differ from the skills needed for decision making. Problem solvers are *searchers* while decision makers are *choosers*. The questions a decision maker must answer are:

1. Given two pieces of information, which shall I base my action on?
2. Given two possible information processors, which shall I use?
3. What particular combination of information and information processors shall I use to increase the probability that I will achieve my goals?

Decision Alternatives

When faced with a choice situation, an individual or group has three alternatives. One is to do nothing, another is to make a personal decision, and the third is to utilize an appropriate decision structure. There are some guidelines to assist managers in determining which strategy should be used in a given situation.

Americans, for the most part, are convinced that the worst thing that the manager can do is nothing. Yet there are times when this is the best strategy available, given the manager's overall task of achieving a desired result. One such time is when all of the available alternatives are disastrous for the system. Although managers can continue to search for other solutions, they should avoid making a choice that will bring harm to the system.

A second instance in which managers should not engage in choice making is when they are clearly not accountable for the outcome and someone else who is accountable is both competent and working on the situation. In this case, getting involved often hurts the situation rather than helps it. Managers can spend too much of their time worrying about the behavior of others in the system when they have no evidence that these others are not meeting their own responsibilities.

The third instance is when no alternative makes a difference to the manager. In this case, it is likely that the choice does make a difference to someone in the organization. The manager should attempt to find that person and let him or her make the decision. This can relieve the manager of what could be a very time-consuming task and can result in a better decision.

It should be obvious from the above discussion that when the manager is advised to do nothing in a decision situation, he or she should not participate in choice making. However, the manager might be engaged in problem solving (finding new alternatives) or delegating authority (getting the choice made by concerned individuals or groups).

Managers are forced to make personal decisions at times. That is, choices are made without benefit of consultation or the involvement of others. This type of situation arises from one of two conditions: first, when the manager cannot share the information; and second, when no appropriate decision structure exists. The second case will become clear in the following section on decision structures. For the moment, it is sufficient to note that sometimes a manager must make a personal decision because there is no appropriate decision structure available.

There are occasions when managers find that they cannot share the information they have with others and must make personal decisions. One reason that managers might not be able to share information is that others in the organization will not understand it. Another is that certain information might be confidential either by law or by custom (certain personnel records, for example). A third reason is that managers may not have time to share the information before they must make a decision. It should be noted, however, that these reasons are also used as excuses to justify decision-making practices that exclude other people. Therefore, the need to make a personal decision must really exist before that prerogative is exercised. A major problem encountered by many college graduates is to recognize a situation where personal decisions are not appropriate, in which case an organizational decision structure should be utilized.

Decision Structures

Bureaucratic, collegial, and political decision systems are the three possible structures that can be used in organizations for decision making. It should be understood that these structures are not separate entities within the organization, but it is useful to analyze them separately.

The bureaucratic decision system is characterized by arrangements of standard information processors dealing with routine information that use clear rules to make routine decisions. Competence in the bureaucratic sense is derived from technical knowledge of the system and the standard operating systems. The managers of McDonald's franchises, bank loan officers, or assembly-line foremen are primarily engaged in routine decision making. There are set rules for choosing between alternatives, and the primary skill involved is fair application of the rules to every situation.

Many companies compete on the basis of their ability to make routine decisions. The better the organizational rules and the more skilled the managers are at applying these rules, the more likely it is that the organization will prosper. Ford competes with General Motors on this basis, as do Sears and Penney's with their competitors and supermarkets with theirs. These are organizations that, as a rule, process routine information and have consequently developed good bureaucratic decision-making structures to help them deal with choice-making situations.

Collegial decision systems are utilized in nonroutine continuous information situations. In a collegial system, the choice is based on a shared value system among those who are concerned with the outcome. Consensus seeking rather than reliance on rules and standard operating procedures is the primary strategy used. The manager is concerned with whether a shared value system can influence a situation and whether the participants are skillful in reaching a consensus. When a patient in a hospital is attended by several physicians, they will meet to discuss and decide treatment using a collegial decision structure. Each physician is interested in his or her speciality, but all have the overriding shared value of the patient's recovery. In this meeting, the doctors discuss the patient's problems and possible treatments at length to reach a consensus on the treatment sequence.

Political decision structures are used in nonroutine discontinuous information situations. The decision made is based on control of resources (including information) and the willingness of the parties affected by the decision situation to use their resources for bargaining. In a political decision situation, a member of the decision structure is involved with determining which participants are concerned about the outcomes of the decision. What resources do concerned individuals or groups control? How willing are they to use these resources? What are their bargaining skills? The answers to these questions give managers information to guide the situation to a constructive resolution. City school boards are excellent examples of political decision structures. Usually elected on the basis of the positions they take on such issues as school budgets, alternative institutional techniques, and mixtures of course offerings, the board members bargain to determine board actions. In a similar fashion the senior management committee of a large multiindustry organization may experience a political decision structure. Managers with different backgrounds and values negotiate the future direction of the company. If a manager's business areas obtain a greater share of the resources, then his stature and the future of his business areas and subordinates become brighter.

Basically, there are three occasions when organizations are faced with nonroutine decision situations and must use collegial or political structures to make choices. The first occasion arises when the organization is faced with scarce resources. Then the organization must answer the question "What are we doing that we can stop?" The second case occurs when the organization has excess resources. The question is "Can we do something that we haven't done before?" The third case develops when the organization feels the need for systems improvement. The fundamental question in this case is "Can we do what we are now doing better?" In each of these situations the organization normally has to make decisions with nonroutine information, and its members must be able to utilize either collegial or political decision structures.

Managers are responsible for developing decision systems as well as for seeing that they are properly utilized. Errors can be made by treating non-routine information as routine and by treating routine information as non-routine. Choosing between collegial and political decision systems becomes a very important task for the manager. If values are shared and the information is nonroutine continuous, then the collegial system is usually appropriate. If values are not shared and the information flow is nonroutine discontinuous, then the political system is generally most useful. In any case, the decision system is one of the resources of the organization and must be skillfully utilized.

Groups as Decision Makers

There is no requirement that consultative decision making be conducted using groups, but all decision structures can use groups as information processors to facilitate the decision process. In a bureaucratic situation, the group brings together those people who have the variety of technical competencies required to make choices. Groups are used to arrive at a consensus in the collegial decision structure. In political situations, the parties to the bargaining situation often meet as a group. It is important, if managers are to manage each situation effectively, that they be aware of the general characteristics of groups as decision makers.

Groups can make different responses to the need to make a decision or to a request that they make a choice between alternatives:

1. By failing to respond at all, the group often forces managers to make personal or private decisions.
2. Groups can try to determine which member knows the most and then support that member's opinion.
3. The group can permit an interested minority to make the decision.
4. The decision can be the result of a majority vote.
5. A group decision can be the average of all individual decisions.
6. The group can require unanimous agreement before reaching a decision.

All six of these strategies are used by groups, and depending on the situation, each can be appropriate.

The question is often asked whether groups make more or less risky decisions than individuals. However, this is not an appropriate question. Groups tend to make decisions that are consistent with culturally held values: When the culture dictates risk, groups will be riskier than individuals; when the generally held cultural value is conservative, groups tend to be more conservative.[12]

There are several advantages of group decision making compared with individual decision making:[13]

1. There is more information.
2. There are more information processing skills.
3. There are more approaches to the decision.
4. There is greater understanding of the decision.

There are also disadvantages to using groups for decision making:[14]

1. Social pressure within the group can lead to perceptual distortion.
2. Individuals may dominate, giving the appearance of a group decision when actually the decision was made by an individual.
3. Clever manipulation of the group can produce a bandwagon effect, where people go along against their better judgment.
4. The group can make a decision that everyone accepts rather than make the best decision for the organization.
5. Groups tend to make a social rather than a technical evaluation of ideas.
6. Group decision making is costly.

Social psychologist Irving Janis, in his dramatic account of several major American foreign policy fiascoes, including the Bay of Pigs invasion, focused on the imperfections of group decision making. He wrote, "Lack of vigilance and excessive risktaking are forms of temporary group derangement to which decision-making groups made up of responsible executives are not at all immune.... Subtle constraints, which the leader may reinforce inadvertently, prevent a member from fully exercising his critical powers and from openly expressing doubts when most others in the group appear to have reached a consensus."[15]

President Kennedy and the White House staff that "approved" the CIA plan to invade Cuba displayed these critical symptoms of "groupthink." According to Janis, the Kennedy advisory group developed "a number of shared illusions and related norms" that significantly affected their perceptions of reality.[16] The symptoms of groupthink attributed to Kennedy's staff include: the illusion of invulnerability, the illusion of unanimity, suppression of personal doubts, and docility fostered by the fear of antagonizing valuable new members.[17] The perceptual selection and distortion that resulted culminated in one of America's major foreign policy disasters.

Summary

This chapter has discussed process following, problem solving, and decision making. Most individuals working in an organization are engaged in all three activities. Workers at the lowest levels perform primarily as process followers (following a predetermined and highly specific path to achieve a desired objective) with limited routine problem solving and decision making; only rarely do they undertake nonroutine problem solving and decision making that might occur as the result of an accident or crisis in their work area.

In today's larger private, governmental, and nonprofit organizations, there are numerous staff groups. Employees in these groups are often hired because of their information processing skills and knowledge in specialized areas, such as law, chemical engineering, contract negotiation, or personnel. These staff professionals perform much process following and problem solving. Their objective in problem solving is to find a path that will achieve the desired output when actual output is deficient. Similar to other information processors, certain selection and distortion characteristics affect the information processing of staff professionals. One possible result may be the termination of a search for alternative paths to the desired output rather than expanded search to find additional paths. This can dramatically influence the alternatives from which the manager (decision maker) chooses. In this situation the staff members are performing problem solving and not decision making, even though their selection and distortion characteristics influence the eventual decision.

Most organizations have relatively few decision makers; they are usually managers at higher levels. Many of the alternatives that managers decide on do not come from their problem-solving activities but are presented from their staffs of professional advisors.

Notes

[1] Herbert A. Simon, *Administrative Behavior* (New York: Macmillan, 1945).

[2] James G. March and Herbert A. Simon, *Organizations* (New York: Wiley, 1958).

[3] Kenyon B. De Greene, *Sociotechnical Systems* (Englewood Cliffs, N.J.: Prentice-Hall, 1973), pp. 33-34.

[4] "Selling Business a Theory of Economies," *Business Week*, September 8, 1973, p. 85.

[5] Ibid.

[6] George A. Steiner and John B. Miner, *Management Policy and Strategy* (New York: Macmillan, 1977), p. 113.

[7] "The Oil Companies Did Spectacularly Last Year. This Year? A Very Different Story." *Forbes*, January 1, 1975, pp. 216–219; "The Mobil Offer That Won Marcor," *Business Week*, August 10, 1974, p. 45.

[8] "Members of the Wedding," *Forbes*, February 15, 1975, p. 33.

[9] "Shipping: A Supertanker Glut Hurts the Market," *Business Week*, November 8, 1974, p. 63.

[10] "Chrysler Digs Itself an Economy Foxhole," *Business Week*, November 30, 1974, p. 24.

[11] Laurence J. Peter and Raymond Hull, *The Peter Principle: Why Things Always Go Wrong* (New York: Morrow, 1969).

[12] J. A. F. Stoner, "Risky and Cautious Shifts in Group Decision: The Influence of Widely-Held Values," *Journal of Experimental Social Psychology*. 1968, *4*, 442–459.

[13] See Douglas R. Bunker and Gene W. Dalton, "The Comparative Effectiveness

of Groups and Individuals in Solving Problems," in *Managing Group and Intergroup Relations,* ed. Jay W. Lorsch and Paul R. Lawrence (Homewood, Ill.: Irwin; 1972), pp. 204–208.

[14] See Joseph A. Litterer, *The Analysis of Organizations,* 2nd ed. (New York: Wiley, 1973), chap. 2.

[15] Irving L. Janis, *Victims of Groupthink* (Boston: Houghton Mifflin, 1972), p. 3.

[16] Ibid., pp. 36–37.

[17] Ibid., pp. 36–48.

The Organization as an Evolving System

9

Introduction

Until now organizations have been perceived as static entities. Yet information flows and the processing that occurs within organizations are increasingly complex. When the structure of the organization is being considered, a multitude of components must be considered simultaneously. The organization is an entity that constantly interacts with its environment, and it has a truly dynamic nature. Ongoing internal processes of the organization combine with environmental forces to create a continuously evolving system.

The first part of this chapter considers aspects of planned and unplanned change and stability. Changes in the organization's environment put pressure on the organization to change. At the same time, organizations are built with negative feedback loops to maintain systems stability. The second part of this chapter looks at organizational conflict and how the organization controls it. Conflict is defined as a breakdown in the standard decision structures within the organization. The third part discusses change as a planned process and the use of feedforward systems to implement change. Change often results from conflict; furthermore, it results in the evolution of inputs and information processors.

Organizations as Changing Systems

Organizational change is any modification that occurs in inputs or processes that causes the outputs of the system to be noticeably different. Figure 9-1 represents the systems model developed in Chapter Four.

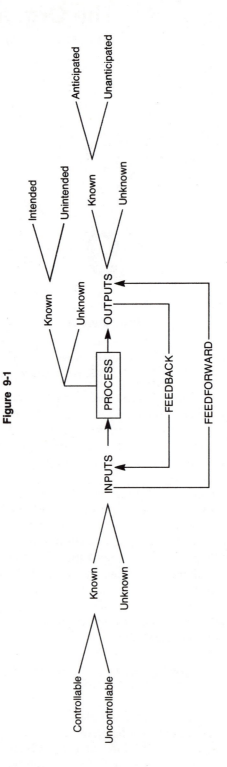

Figure 9-1

Systems change is of concern to individuals and groups in an organization because they need to know how a variation in I_1 or the I.P. affects the altered outputs, which we will designate I_2'. If systems change is undesirable, that is, if I_2' does not match the desired results, then the organization is interested in introducing either control adjustments into the system to cause I_2' to return to its initial state (I_2) or planned change to move the system to a new, desired state (I_2'').

Planned and Unplanned Change

Planned change is the purposeful manipulation of controllable input variables and intended process variables to cause the known output variable to be significantly different from what it was before the manipulation. It is likely that before planned change can occur, some systems inputs must be moved from the unknown to the known or from the uncontrolled to the controlled categories. It may also be likely that some unintended processing must be more fully understood and perhaps brought into the category of intended processing.

Planned change utilizes problem-solving and decision-making processes. Recognizing the need for planned change and executing it consists of four stages:

1. The actual I_2 outputs are not the desired outputs.
2. Problem solving consists of finding a path to achieve the desired outputs by altering either the inputs or the information processors.
3. Decision making consists of choosing from alternative paths.
4. Change implementation consists of moving the system to a new path.

The following examples will illustrate the concept of planned change. A consumer products firm has yearly model changes. Therefore, in the case of a dress manufacturer, the organization will bring in new inputs in terms of materials, change information processors, and thus create new desired products, the styles for the new fall season. This occurs after the organization comes up with alternatives in the problem-solving phase and then decides on preferred styles.

Another example of a planned change occurs when an organization decides to implement a 10 percent cost reduction to maintain its competitiveness and to increase the market for its product. The problem-solving process determines alternative ways to cut costs by changing either materials used in the product, the quantity of materials used, or the way the product is manufactured. In the decision-making phase, the organization accepts or rejects the alternatives developed.

Another planned change would be where a firm finds that the actual volume of output does not equal the desired volume of output. The problem-solving process develops several production expansion plans. Either the most desirable one is selected in the decision-making phase, or the decision is made not to expand the plant. If a plan is approved for expansion, the change implementation process brings additional supplies into the organization and alters the arrangement of the organizational structure to increase plant capacity.

Planned change can be as simple as the replacement of personnel. When the plant manager leaves, the actual output does not equal the desired output, which in this case is a fully staffed organization. Information on the departure of the plant manager is anticipated by the feedforward system that forecasts a planned retirement, or it can be recognized by the feedback system through the resignation or unexpected death of the plant manager. The problem-solving process determines possible candidates for the position, and one of these candidates is selected in the decision process. The change is implemented when the new plant manager takes over his or her duties.

Planned change requires special attention to the feedback loops in the system. Systems ability to carry out planned change and its problem-solving component is a function of the care and maintenance of feedback loops.

While this section is concerned primarily with planned change, it is important to note that continual unplanned change occurs within organizations, when, for example, an I_1' or I.P.'—which were not decided on and implemented by the manager—produce an undesirable I_2'. In today's complex world there is a continual stream of new, uncontrollable, unknown alterations in inputs. In addition, there exists unknown or unintended processing by the technical and human information processors, which produce outputs that are unanticipated or unknown by management.

Unplanned change occurs when $I_2' \neq I_2$. The manager may determine that the I_2' is preferable to I_2. When this occurs, the outcome is beneficial. For example, a supplier can alter the chemical composition of a plastic part (I_1') for a toy manufacturer without informing the producer. The resulting output (I_2') is a stronger toy with fewer rejects. Thus, the new I_2' is preferred by the manager of the toy manufacturer, and the result is an unplanned, desirable change.

Alternatively, the unplanned change could result in an I_2' that is inferior to the old output (I_2). In this case, the feedback system tells the manager that $I_2' \neq I_2$ and that the I_2' is not desired. The organization then enters a series of problem-solving, decision-making, and control-adjustment behaviors to determine what I_1' or I.P.' is causing the changed I_2' and to assess what can be done to return $I_2' \rightarrow I_2$. For example, a production group within the toy manufacturer might become disgruntled with the company and consciously leave one part out of every fifth toy (I.P.'). The result is an increase in the rejects; the I_2' is inferior to I_2. Through feedback the organization becomes aware of the increase in rejects. The system consequently initiates problem-solving, decision-making, and control-adjustment behavior to determine why $I_2' \neq I_2$. When the processes are successful, the manager selects and implements a path to return the system to the old state, $I_2' \rightarrow I_2$.

Systems Control,
Stability, and Resistance to Change

A distinction needs to be made between systems control and systems change. Both systems control and systems change go through four similar steps. First is using feedback loops for problem recognition where actual I_2 $\neq$ desired I_2. Second is problem solving, which is finding paths to achieve the desired I_2. Third is decision making, which is choosing from alternative paths. For systems control, the decision-making choice returns the system to the old inputs I_1 and previous known and intended information processes I.P. Alternatively, in systems change, the decision-making choice moves the system to altered inputs I_1 and/or modified information processes I.P. Fourth is moving the system to the chosen path; control adjustments return the system to the old state, and change implementations move the system to the new state.

In most organizations considerable effort is made to provide feedback loops that will give the information necessary to maintain systems control. Most successful organizations are effective at maintaining systems stability, using something such as systems control. Rapid and efficient systems control makes organizations very resistant to change. For example, a production group can develop a production process that increases productivity. Without telling the plant manager, the group implements the change I.P. $\rightarrow$ I.P.' Unfortunately, at least in the initial implementation, the change to I.P.' reduces the quality of the product as well as increases the number of units produced (I_2'). The quality control group, noting the lower quality of the product, sets in motion the systems control, which results in control adjustments so that the production workers return to their old production process. A conflict between the production and quality control groups could result; that is, the change could lead to a conflict management problem (see Figure 9-2).

Organizations increase in size by increasing the number of component groups. As organizational size increases, it becomes more difficult for one group to unilaterally make a change that alters its output, since that output represents an input for one or more of the other groups in the organization. Systems control attempts to return the system to the old state. The strength of the control functions leads to resistance to change, which is commonly encountered when dealing with large organizations.

It is this tremendous resistance to change that makes change management important in today's rapidly changing society. The inability of organizations to make timely changes often leads to their eventual failure; the histories of Packard Motor Company, Penn Central Railroad, W. T. Grant,

Figure 9-2. Systems Control Reaction to Unplanned Change

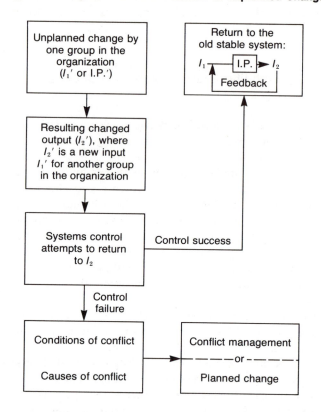

and Merchant Calculators are examples of this. It has also been observed that often a new or small organization is more tolerant of change and more willing to develop or to accept radically new ideas. Large organizations have stimulated radical change by establishing totally new entities rather than changing their existing structures. These new ventures operate independently with minimal interaction with groups in the established organizations.

Conflict within an Organization

Chapter Eight has shown that organizations have standard ways of making decisions. Many of these standard decision-making procedures require the interaction of two or more people who must agree on a particular choice so that the organization can act. The managerial function of choosing an alternative for the organization was defined as decision making. Chapter Eight also includes a discussion about the possible structures that can be utilized by managers in organizations to accomplish the tasks associated with decision making. These are bureaucratic, collegial, and political decision structures. Conflict is a breakdown in the standard methods of decision making within each of these decision structures. It causes individuals, groups, or organizations difficulty in choosing an active alternative.[1] For example, after a decision has been reached by a group, a member can exert pressure on the group to reconsider and change the decision.

Conditions of Conflict and Competition

Four conditions are necessary for conflict and competition in organizations:[2]

1. *Two or more parties:* Two or more parties are concerned with the choice of an action alternative.
2. *A common field* (frame of reference): There exists a set of rules that defines or constrains the future activity of the two parties.
3. *Outcome preference:* The parties think that they might be better (or worse) off in some future state if a particular alternative is chosen.
4. *Awareness:* The parties are aware of what is going on.

Managers in organizations are concerned with conflict and competition; they are also concerned with the conditions necessary for competition and conflict to develop. Competition and conflict are natural and occur frequently, especially today, when complex organizations are composed of people from a great variety of backgrounds with different goals and perceptions of the world. Once the conditions of conflict and competition are present, it is the ability of the organization's decision system to handle the resulting confrontation that determines whether competition or conflict will develop. One strategy is to manage the four conditions that cause competition and conflict.

Conflict and competition can develop between individuals, groups, or organizations. For example, conflict tends to develop between different functional units in the organization. This observation can be illustrated by focusing on the decision processes of a large manufacturing firm that produces agricultural implements. The product design group and the production division of the firm might not agree on specific aspects of a farm implement. Product design continually presses for more time and financial resources to perfect a technically complex design. Production prefers a simpler design that is easier to manufacture. The same situation applies to relations between production and marketing. In addition to the desire to produce simple farm implements, production prefers to schedule its production runs on a stable, consistent basis, for example, equal production runs for every month of the year. Marketing, however, requires that a supply of implements be available for those periods of the year when most implements are sold. These same types of problems can develop between marketing and field services and between field services and product design.

Conflict and competition always exist in an organization because the perceptions, abilities, and interests of the various subsystems differ. The product designer strives to design a perfect product, whereas financial management and the sales force want something to produce and sell that generates revenues and profits. The design group wants the ultimate in product sophistication, whereas the financial people want a product with the lowest possible production cost that still provides the features customers need. The salesmen want to sell whatever the customer wants, regardless of whether it requires design or production changes. The production people want the fewest special features offered on a standard product so that there will be minimal production changes.

Conflict between functional units is caused by a breakdown in the organization's standard decision-making processes, making it difficult for the organization to choose an action alternative to such questions as the following:

1. What should this product be like?
2. How large an inventory should the organization carry?
3. How important should the availability of replacement parts be?
4. How many special versions of the product should the organization make?

Control of Information to Reduce Conflict and Competition

When managers are aware of the conditions of competition and conflict between two groups, they can sometimes reduce their impact by managing the information that is available. They can (1) keep the two groups from knowing about each other, (2) keep the two groups from knowing that they cannot both be right, (3) arrange the activities of the two groups so that the groups will not be in direct competition, and (4) direct the attention of the two groups away from each other (for example, toward an outside competitor).

There are many examples illustrating how information is used to eliminate or reduce conflict and competition in organizations. Two research groups unknown to each other might be set up to develop a new widget using different technologies. A capital-budgeting process could be established in which the total amount eventually spent by each group is not made known until after all projects are submitted. A second example is where a new product development process, indicating a clear sequence of phases with well-defined responsibilities for each phase, could be specified. A third example is to divert the attention of the research, manufacturing, and marketing groups away from each other and toward the new product being created by a competitor.

The primary technique used by the manager to reduce or eliminate the conditions of conflict and competition is the design of the organization. Organizational structure determines the division of operating groups, their specified goals and objectives, the individual task descriptions, and the information system used to evaluate the individuals and groups. Control of information relating to goals, tasks, and performance can be used to reduce or eliminate conditions of conflict and competition. The manager and members of each group within the organization arrive at goals and objectives for their group either explicitly or implicitly. It is usually desirable for the manager and the group to have similar goals and objectives, although they seldom are identical. For example, the manager might see high productivity, quality control, and lower production costs as the desired group goals. The members' goals might be not working too hard, making sure the work day is over at exactly 5:00 p.m., and meeting at the neighborhood bar at 5:15 for a beer.

Information in the organization specifies the goals and objectives of the various groups and individuals. Similarly, information structures the work environment through formal job descriptions that specify the requirements and duties of each job and how it is to be performed. The organization evaluates employees, including managers, and provides rewards and incentives, such as pay raises and bonuses; it also provides punishments, such as firing, no promotions, and demotions. These mechanisms are used to encourage the work groups and employees to accomplish their stated goals and objectives and to perform their jobs as specified in their position descriptions.

To reduce the conditions of conflict and competition, the work environment is structured so that each subgroup is an independent processing entity. Another way of stating this is to say that one group's processing—including its perceived tasks and rewards for performing these tasks—is relatively independent of another group's processing. Stated in systems terms, this means that the manager wants to make all the inputs from other parts of the organization to a particular group known and controlled, the feedback systems formal and negative, and the rewards to the individuals in the group independent of the uncontrollable input from other parts of the organization.

The manager can design the organization to limit the potential conflict caused by the interface problems between departments, such as product design, production, marketing, and field services, by developing goals and objectives, task descriptions, and evaluation mechanisms for each group (see Figure 9-3). There is often an effort to create self-contained tasks and independent units.[3] Functional interdependencies limit this approach, but often the manager can develop ways of managing these interdependencies and accomplishing organizational goals.

Figure 9-3. Techniques to Reduce Conflict and Competition within an Organization

Department	Goals and Objectives	Task Description	Performance Evaluation
Product Design	Product specifications such as performance, cost to manufacture, quality, and serviceability	Nonroutine descriptions	Meeting specifications and schedule
Production	Production targets and standard costs with allowances made for costs and delays due to setups, short runs, and new models	Routine descriptions	Actual production costs vs. objectives
Marketing	Sales quotas (targets) based on historical experience and market analysis	Routine descriptions	Actual sales vs. quota
Field Services	Time standards for each type of service call	Routine descriptions	Actual service time vs. standards, complaints

By controlling the flow of information and the specifications and evaluation of human information processors, the organization tries to reduce three of the conditions of conflict and competition. First, the condition where two or more parties are concerned with the choice of an action alternative has been reduced by making the goals and objectives of the groups independent of each other. Second, the condition where a common field exists has been reduced by detailed job descriptions, which define very different job fields for each group and which also define information flows between the groups. Third, the outcome preference condition has been reduced by the evaluation procedure, which makes each group's rewards independent of the decisions of the other groups in the organization.

Competition or Conflict

Conditions for competition and conflict exist in every organization; managers might not be able, or want, to eliminate them. For example, a manager who wants the sales groups in different geographical regions to increase their sales levels will tolerate situations of conflict and competition. To deal with ubiquitous conditions of conflict and competition, the manager tries to structure the organization's information and decision-making system so that competition rather than conflict results.

The difference between competition and conflict is important. The organization's decision system can arrive at a decision in a competitive situation; the parties accept the decision and move to the next activity, even though there is a strong outcome preference by each of the groups. Conflict results in a breakdown in the standard methods of decision making within the organization's decision structure; the parties involved do not accept the decision, and they expend energy to change it.

A few examples of competitive situations follow. A company anticipates a very tough year and needs to cut expenses in order to remain profitable. The conditions of conflict and competition are present; each component group of the company argues that the other groups are less essential and wants to cut the staff and budgets of other groups and preserve their own. The potential conflict adds further strain to the already poor business environment of the firm. In this case, it is not possible to eliminate the conditions of conflict and competition. However, it might be possible to obtain an agreement in the decision system and thereby create a competitive atmosphere within the firm. The manager can attempt to persuade all the groups to agree to across-the-board budget cuts of, for example, 10 percent. The groups are then evaluated on their actual savings, with special bonuses to the group producing the largest savings.

A second company has four divisions, each of which operates as a separate business. All divisions are critically interested in the corporate decision to allocate money for investment, which creates conditions for conflict and competition. A competitive environment can be encouraged by communicating investment selection criteria and then obtaining a consensus from the four decision managers on its reasonability.

Conflict Management Framework

To better understand situations where conflict occurs, it is useful to consider a conflict management framework (Figure 9-4), which summarizes the material presented in this chapter. It shows that when the conditions for conflict and competition are present, the manager can attempt either to reduce the conditions for conflict or to create competition through the control of information. If the manager is unable to do either, conflict will occur. Conflict within an organization is disruptive and costly, consuming an enormous amount of time and energy. Participants in the conflict situation are hindered in their efforts to perform their normal functions.

March and Simon's classic framework for conflict identifies the three major causes:[4]

1. a felt need for joint decision making in a situation where there are no provisions for joint decision making
2. differences in perception such that the two parties see the same situation so differently that they are unable to make choices together
3. differences in goals such that the two parties want such different outcomes from the situation that they are unable to make choices together

A bureaucratic decision system, discussed in Chapter Eight, is characterized by arrangements of standard information processors dealing with routine information and utilizing clear rules to make routine decisions.

Figure 9-4. Conflict Management Framework

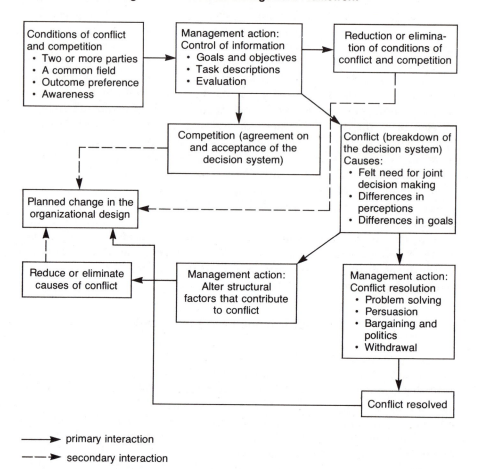

——————▶ primary interaction

— — — ▶ secondary interaction

Conflict in a bureaucratic organization results when a breakdown in standard operating procedures occurs. In such a situation, a felt need for joint decision making exists, but there are no provisions or clear rules available to make the required decision.

Collegial decision systems, utilizing nonroutine continuous information, base their decisions on values and goals that are shared by those parties concerned with the outcomes. Differences in perception, such that the concerned parties see the decision situation so differently that they are unable to make choices together, result in conflict.

Political structures, utilizing nonroutine discontinuous information flows where there are differences in values and goals, base their decisions on the control of organizational resources and on the willingness of parties affected by the choice situation to utilize their own resources for bargaining. Conflict in a political system occurs when such differences in goals exist that the concerned parties want outcomes so different from each other that they are unable to make choices together.

Figure 9-5 presents the decision systems usually associated with the different types of information flows and the primary cause of conflict in each.

Figure 9-5

Information Flow	Decision System	Primary Conflict Cause
Routine	Bureaucratic	Felt need for joint decision making
Nonroutine Continuous	Collegial	Differences in perception
Nonroutine Discontinuous	Political	Differences in goals

Another strategy evolving from the conflict management framework is management of the structural factors contributing to the three causes of conflict. The structural conflict framework, depicted in Figure 9-6, is an extension of the hypothesis proposed by March and Simon. Figure 9-6 presents some of the factors within an organization that affect conflict. It also indicates that if there is an increase in any one of these three causes of conflict (the other two remaining constant), there will be an increase in the conflict between the groups or subsystems of the organization.

Consider the example of a street vendor business and some changes that could occur. Initially, the street vendor designs, manufactures, sells, and services handicrafts without any assistance. As the vendor's business expands to become an organization, the following might occur: Suborganizations to design and manufacture are added, and there is an increase in the organization's division of labor. The division of labor is also accompanied

Figure 9-6. Causes of Structural Conflict in an Organization

Felt need for joint decision making increases as:	Differences in perception increase as:	Differences in group goals increase as:
• predictability of the environmental inputs decreases • standardization of inputs and processes decreases • specialization of processes increases • interdependency in timing between processes increases • mutual dependence on scarce resources increases	• division of labor increases • number of independent information sources increases • handling of information increases • differences in time perspectives increase • number of different sources of information increases	• shared resources become more scarce • differences in individual goals increase • organizational goals become less operational • the reward system becomes more competitive

by an increase in the number of independent information sources. Adding new design and manufacturing groups in different physical locations to different knowledge and skill requirements increases the number of different sources of information. These two structural factors tend to increase differences in perception.

When the street vendor adds design and manufacturing groups, there is an increase in the difference in time perspectives, which becomes evident as the new design group thinks about sales one year from now and the manufacturing group is interested in sales today and tomorrow. The difference in time perspectives tends to increase the difference in perceptions, which in turn represents a cause of conflict. As the differences in perception increase, so do the chances of conflict.

For a second example, consider the typical state university from 1958 to 1978. In 1958 state universities were well financed, receiving large increases in their yearly budgets and growing rapidly. Most state universities now find resources less plentiful. Also, the number of different groups, departments, and educational programs has increased. Mutual dependence on scarce resources tends to increase the difference in goals that the groups have, thus increasing the chances of conflict.

Figure 9-6 indicates that the operationality of organizational goals influences the differences in goals. By an operational goal is meant a goal that is precisely defined. For example, if a university wants to graduate 1,000 students with bachelor of arts degrees per year and spend no more than $4 million, it has an operational goal. Goals for educational excellence or for superior productivity in research are not operational. Thus, as organizational goals are defined more specifically, they become more operational and a decrease in differences in goals results. State universities over the last twenty years have decreased the differences in goals between groups by going to more goals that are operational, specifying quantity rather than quality, such as the number of students to be graduated and the amount of money to be allotted to budgets.

The framework that has been presented provides a partial list of structural factors that could generate conflict in an organization. In some situations it is possible to alter one of these structural factors and reduce the cause of conflict. For example, most consumer product firms periodically eliminate low-volume or overlapping products to create greater standardization. This tends to reduce the felt need for decision making and thus lessens the likelihood of conflict occurring between groups within the organization.

Conflict—A Signal for Change

Chapters Six and Seven discussed the problem of complexity in organizations. Increases in complexity result from an increasing number of systems linkages and the increasingly hierarchical structure of contemporary organizations. This complexity generates the structural factors (shown in Figure 9-6) that increase the causes of conflict. The manager can partially control the linkages between the information processors in the organization and thereby reduce the felt need for joint decision making. If the manager is not able to reduce the conditions of conflict, he or she will also find that it is difficult to reduce the remaining two causes of conflict: differences in group perceptions and differences in group goals. But conflict is not always avoidable. It often signals that the decision system of an organization needs reevaluation and change, and thus it serves as a stimulus for change.

Conflict most often occurs where groups exchange information. A breakdown in the standard ways of making decisions occurs when the information is processed by personnel who have (1) a particular perception of the world, (2) a limited cognitive capability, (3) limited problem-solving skills, or (4) the need to make decisions. When the product design chief meets with the manufacturing manager, when there are discussions between the sales force and the service personnel group, or when there are interactions between the bank's internal auditor and the bank's accountant, conflict can be expected to occur.

Conflict Resolution

The final alternative proposed in the conflict management framework (see Figure 9-4) is to attack the cause of conflict. In order to do this, the organization resolves its immediate conflict and establishes a new decision system to handle recurring conflict situations. Four major processes are utilized by organizations in their reactions to conflict. These reactions include problem solving, persuasion, bargaining and "politics,"[5] and withdrawal.

Conflict is the breakdown of the organization's standard decision structure. Conflict resolution both resolves the current inability for groups to reach a decision and also changes the standard decision structure and the methods of decision making to eliminate the current cause of conflict. Figure 9-7 illustrates the relationship between the three most likely causes of conflict in the three decision structures and the likely conflict resolution techniques generally employed to handle the conflicts. Again, it is important to stress that any of the techniques could be used, as Figure 9-7 indicates.

Problem Solving   Problem solving has been thoroughly discussed in Chapter Eight. Utilization of this conflict resolution technique assumes that objectives are shared by concerned organizational participants in a problem-solving situation. The decision problem is basically one of identifying a solution that satisfies the shared criteria of the participants. In problem solv-

Figure 9-7.   Use of Different Conflict Resolution Techniques by Decision Structures

Decision Structure	Cause of Conflict	Conflict Resolution Technique			
		Problem Solving	Persuasion	Bargaining and "Politics"	Withdrawal
Bureaucratic	Felt need for joint decision making	Primary	Occasional	Occasional	Secondary
Collegial	Differences in perception	Occasional	Primary	Occasional	Secondary
Political	Differences in goals	Occasional	Occasional	Primary	Secondary

ing, the importance of gathering information is emphasized, search behavior is intensified, and the generation of new alternatives is emphasized.

Persuasion   Individuals or groups in the organization are assumed to hold objectives or information that are different but not fixed. Implicit in the use of persuasion is the belief that at some level in the organization, objectives are shared but that the information available to the groups is different. Reference to these shared objectives is utilized to mediate disagreements over subgoals, and the nature of the difference in perception is explored through competing arguments. Testing the subgoals for consistency with other organizational objectives is emphasized, as are the validity and usefulness of existing information. As a result, fewer organizational resources are devoted to gathering new information.

Bargaining and "Politics"   Individuals or groups are assumed to hold objectives that are different and fixed. The rules of bargaining are taken as fixed by the participants. The arena of the bargaining process includes (1) acknowledged conflicts of interest, (2) threats, (3) falsification of positions, and (4) gamesmanship.

"Politics" is the extreme form of bargaining. In the area of "politics," the rules of bargaining are not considered to be fixed by the participants. There are "no holds barred" in seeking solutions. This type of conflict resolution leads to a decision about the current issue but also generally leads to a permanent change in the organization's decision system.

Withdrawal   A final solution to a conflict is the physical withdrawal of a key individual or group. Withdrawal can occur involuntarily; for instance, the manager, after attempting the other three methods of conflict resolution and failing, can fire key members of a group. Withdrawal can also occur voluntarily where key individuals quit. With one or more of the conflicting parties gone, the conflict dissolves. Most managers consider withdrawal to be the least desirable form of conflict resolution; however, as more of today's organizations become collegial and political decision systems, withdrawal is becoming more frequent. A university mathematics department will split apart and become separate departments of mathematics and statistics. A professional firm, composed of lawyers, engineers, or computer consultants, will find that its "young Turks" are leaving to establish their own firm. A voluntary society interested in conservation will split to form a new organization which has a specific conservation cause that the older society is unwilling to support.

Conflict resolution occurs through the management of standard decision-making systems. It is one of the reasons that managers change information processing systems in their organizations.

Managers who spend too much time trying to avoid conflict—either the conditions or the causes—are probably mismanaging their decision systems. This observation stems from the fact that conflict in organizations cannot be completely eliminated. First, the conditions of conflict cannot always be avoided. Second, eliminating the causes of conflict can subvert other organizational goals. Third, information will always be managed by imperfect systems.

It is often assumed that conflict in organizations is bad and should be avoided. Unfortunately, conflict cannot be avoided; managers must learn to live with it and manage it.

Changing Human Behavior
in the Organization

A discussion of changing human behavior in the organization could focus on several levels within the organizational hierarchy. For example, the corporate executives who perform the problem solving and decision making for a plant relocation might perceive the change very differently from the local plant management and production workers who must relocate or lose their jobs. In this section, the framework will allow consideration of change at both levels.

The taxonomy used here to understand strategies for change is a modification of the taxonomy developed by Robert Chin and Kenneth D. Benne.[6] They suggest three change strategies: rational-empirical, normative-reeducative, and power-coercive. For each strategy we will give basic assumptions, conditions of use, and examples. In the initial discussion of these concepts, we are referring to the individual or group that manages the change situation.

Rational-empirical change strategies assume that people are guided by reason and will follow their rational self-interest once it is revealed to them. Normative-reeducative change strategies assume that people are not fully able to understand what is most appropriate and are therefore guided by value systems communicated through social norms and institutions. Power-coercive change strategies assume that it is necessary to apply legal, economic, moral, and other types of sanctions to get people to change. Each of these assumptions is true to some extent; the degree to which they apply depends on the situation.

The first and the most important factor in selecting a change strategy is to look at the information flow connected with the change situation. If the information flow is routine, then the information is easily understood, familiar, repetitive, relatively fixed, and patterned. In such a situation, people are likely to be guided by reason. Figure 9-8 summarizes how the group involved in making the change should determine its selection of a change strategy.

Figure 9-8. Selection of a Change Strategy

Strategy	Information	Value Questions	Magnitude of Change	Time Pressure
Rational-Empirical	Routine	Small	Small	Small
Normative-Reeducative	Nonroutine Continuous	Moderate	Moderate	Moderate
Power-Coercive	Nonroutine Discontinuous	Large	Large	Large

If, however, the information flow is either nonroutine continuous or nonroutine discontinuous, then the information flow is not understood, unfamiliar, not repetitive, not fixed, and not patterned. Under these conditions, it is likely that the assumptions underlying normative-reeducative or power-coercive change strategies will hold.

The second factor in selecting a change strategy becomes evident as the manager looks at the value questions surrounding the change. If there is no demand that people change their value systems in order to accommodate the change, then they are likely to accept a rational basis. If, however, some moderate changes in value position are required, then a normative-reeducative change strategy is appropriate. When there is a requirement that people make a major shift in value position, it is unlikely that they will respond to any change strategy except power-coercive.

The third factor is the magnitude of the change. If the change is relatively minor, requiring only a small shift in behavior, then rational-empirical change strategies seem appropriate. When the change is more moderate, requiring a significant shift in behavior but not affecting fundamental patterns, then normative-reeducative strategies are useful. On those occasions when a person or group must fundamentally restructure their behavior, power-coercive change strategies are required.

The fourth factor is the time frame one has for accomplishing the change. Rational-empirical strategies take a long time and are therefore most useful when there is little or no urgency in the situation. Normative-reeducative strategies are useful under conditions of moderate urgency. When change must be accomplished quickly and abruptly, power-coercive strategies are most appropriate.

Examples of rational-empirical change strategies include general education, content-oriented staff training, trade literature, systems analysis, applied research, and suggestion systems.

Examples of normative-reeducative change strategies include outside management and technical consultants, staff technical groups, hiring personnel with new skills and knowledge, cross-functional management committees, special task forces, and psychotherapy, counseling, and other psychological change techniques.

Examples of power-coercive change strategies include government regulation, formal authority or power, legal and court processes, statutory law, economic boycott, and war.

In today's large organizations, the hierarchical level at which the problem solving, decision making, and planned change occur is often controlled by the organization's management. For example, a change in the organization's production process could be made by different groups in the organization: the work group, the industrial engineering group, or the plant management group. Often the manager will carefully consider the change situation and then select the group that will be given the responsibility and authority for the change. The manager will consider sources of knowledge on the problem and the problem solution and seek out the group that has such knowledge.

There is evidence that when a group must change, its willingness to change will increase if it is allowed to participate in the change rather than if it is thrust into the change by a power-coercive strategy.

The problem of managing change within the organization today is important; it will often be specified as part of the goals, objectives, and task descriptions of groups within the organization. The production group is expected to develop and implement changes that alter their outputs, such as increasing productivity, decreasing scrap, or decreasing machinery downtime. A product development group might have as its entire focus the development of the company's yearly model changes as well as the creation and introduction of new products. Often temporary groups, the most popular being committees, are established to serve as the change managers. The committee can provide additional problem-solving ability, as discussed in Chapter Eight, and bring together representatives of the groups that will be affected by the change as a result of the committee's decision. The selection of a change strategy used by a group will depend on the information system, value questions, magnitude of the change, and time frame of the change. Examples of group perceptions regarding these three change strategies are provided in Figure 9-9.

The management of systems change is largely a function of the manager's ability to execute planned change. As in the case of the group, the

Figure 9-9. Group Perceptions of Change Strategies

Change	Change Manager	Reference Group	Reference Group's Perceptions				
			Information	Value Questions	Magnitude	Pressure	Strategy
Plant Relocation	Corporate management in large multiplant firm	Corporate management	Nonroutine continuous	Moderate	Moderate	Moderate	Normative-reeducative
Plant Relocation	Corporate management in large multiplant firm	Plant work group	Nonroutine discontinuous	Large	Large	Large	Power-coercive
Solid Waste Regulation	Corporate management of manufacturing firm with much solid waste	Corporate management	Nonroutine discontinuous	Large	Large	Large	Power-coercive
New Equipment Lubrication Schedule	Manufacturing group	Manufacturing group	Routine	Small	Small	Small	Rational-empirical
Model Year Change	New product development group in a large corporation	New product development group	Nonroutine continuous	Moderate	Moderate	Moderate	Normative-reeducative
Model Year Change	New product development group in a large corporation	Manufacturing group	Routine	Small	Small	Moderate	Rational-empirical
Computerization of Accounting System	Independent consultant assisted by accounting group	Corporate management	Mostly routine	Small	Small	Small	Rational-empirical
Computerization of Accounting System	Independent consultant assisted by accounting group	Professional accounting group	Nonroutine continuous	Moderate	Moderate to large	Moderate	Normative-reeducative
Computerization of Accounting System	Independent consultant assisted by accounting group	Clerical staff	Nonroutine discontinuous	Large	Large	Large	Power-coercive

manager's ability to execute planned change is a function of his or her ability to understand the information system, the value questions, the magnitude of change, and the time frame of change.

Notes

[1] James G. March and Herbert A. Simon, *Organizations* (New York: Wiley, 1958), p. 112.

[2] Morton Deutsch, "A Theory of Co-Operation and Competition," *Human Relations*, 1949, *2*, 129–152.

[3] Jay Galbraith, *Organizational Design* (Reading, Mass.: Addison-Wesley, 1977), p. 85.

[4] March and Simon, *Organizations*, p. 121.

[5] Ibid., p. 129.

[6] Robert Chin and Kenneth D. Benne, "General Strategies for Effecting Changes in Human Systems," in *The Planning of Change*, 2nd ed., ed. Warren G. Bennis, Kenneth D. Benne, and Robert Chin (New York: Holt, Rinehart and Winston, 1969), pp. 32–59.

Organizational Theory: An Information Perspective

10

Introduction

As organizations continue to assume a more prominent role in the structure of our society, it becomes more important that we understand as much as possible about their nature, structure, and management. The information systems perspective developed in this book attempts to facilitate such an understanding. Our intent has been to increase the reader's knowledge of organizational design and ability to manage the ongoing operations of the organization.

Organizational design is discussed in the first part of this chapter. This is the process by which the boundaries of a system are determined and the basic elements of the system are specified: its inputs, information processors, outputs, and feedback and feedforward loops. The second part presents a summary of the five basic organizational functions—process following, problem solving, decision making, conflict management, and change management—as they relate to the flow of information in an organization.

Organizational Design

Organizational design addresses a question of procedure, of how to put together the available resources to get the desired results. The question is easy to ask but not easy to answer. People always want to know the specific set of rules used to arrange the various parts of the organization. Since the fit of components looks logical, it is often assumed that there is a specific way to design the organization. Some people think that putting together an organization is like putting together a jigsaw puzzle. But organizational design is much more like painting a picture or writing a song; there is no one solution nor is there one arrangement of parts that is essential. Organizational design does not start completely from scratch, either. Just as a painter must have certain materials and skills, so must the organizational designer have certain kinds of knowledge.

Before an organizational design is attempted, the designers must have an idea about what is needed and desired. The idea is generated from the designer's experiences and his or her heuristic ability. While the idea might lack precise definition, particularly in the early stages of development, it must exist. It is an *idea* that forms the nucleus around which all design revolves.

Once the designer has an idea, he or she needs two kinds of knowledge in order to begin to translate the idea into the organization. The first kind is general conceptual knowledge, which guides the design of any organization. The second kind is specific industry knowledge, which is necessary to execute the specific idea with which the designer is working.

These knowledge requirements are met by answering the following four questions:

1. What are the key elements necessary?
2. What are the basic parameters required?
3. What are the basic functions required?
4. What is the nature and scope of the interactions between the key elements, the basic parameters, and the basic functions?

Industry Knowledge of Organizational Design   It is beyond the scope of this book to convey the specific industry understanding needed to design an organization successfully. A moment's reflection will reveal the wide variety of knowledge required to develop a particular kind of organization. However, the characteristics of a specific organization can be separated into two groups:

1. *General industry bodies of knowledge:* These are concepts that are applicable to all entities and that can be identified both through the organization's placement under a major, intermediate, or specific activity category (see Figure 10-1) and through the degree of profit regulation and government control to which the organization is subject.
2. *Specific organization bodies of knowledge:* These concepts are not applicable to any other entity; they are unique to a particular organization.

Figure 10-1.   Industry Diversity

Degree of Profit Regulation and Government Control	Major Activity Category[a]	Intermediate Activity Category[a]	Specific Activity Category[a]
Less Regulated Business	Agriculture Forestry Fishing Mining Manufacturing Wholesale trade	Food Tobacco Textiles Lumber Paper Chemicals	Alkalis Acetylene Copper chloride Nickel sulfate Sulfuric acid Nylon fibers Antibiotics
More Regulated Business	Finance Insurance Transportation Communication Electrical services	Federal Reserve Banks Commercial, stock, and savings banks Savings and loan associations Personnel credit	State banks (members of Federal Reserve) State Banks (not members of Federal Reserve) National banks Trust companies Unincorporated private banks
Nonprofit Organizations	Education Hospitals Membership organizations Churches	Elementary and secondary schools Colleges and universities Library information centers Correspondence schools	Centers for documentation Circulating libraries Lending libraries Book rental
Governments	Federal State County District	Executive and general government Justice, public order, and safety Public finance and taxation Human resource programs Economic programs	Courts Police Legal counsel and prosecution Correctional institutions Fire protection

[a]A partial list selected from over hundreds of industrial groups in the *Standard Industrial Classification Manual–1972*, Office of Management and Budget, Executive Office of the President (Washington, D.C.: U.S. Government Printing Office, 1972).

Source: Edward L. Summers and Kenneth E. Knight, *Management Advisory Services by CPA's, A Study of Required Knowledge* (New York: American Institute of Certified Public Accountants, 1976), p. 53. Copyright © 1976 by the American Institute of Certified Public Accountants, Inc. Reprinted by permission.

Industry knowledge refers to the specialized concepts required to design retail, communications, manufacturing, financial, insurance, utility, and other categories of organizations. These organizations operate for profit in a relatively regulated free enterprise environment, along with government and nonprofit institutions in the public sector. Some industry concepts are relatively enduring; others can change rapidly as the structure or definition of industry categories evolves or as basic technologies, government regulations, and unique supply and demand situations evolve. Even though specialized industry knowledge is important in organizational design, it is impossible to identify the unique industry knowledge associated with each industry and with each firm. Several categories that include much of the precise industry knowledge required for organizational design are specified in the following list.

1. *Major purpose:* an understanding of the major processes by which private industry seeks to earn profits or an understanding of the functions, services, or processes of public sector organizations

2. *Market structure:* degree of concentration and competition in the markets in which the organization participates as buyer or seller, including capital, raw materials, labor, finished goods or services, by-products, and so forth

3. *External variables:* major economic, political, and legal trends and problems affecting the industry's markets

4. *Technologies and practices:* broad outlines of technologies and management practices used by the industry and the significance of anticipated changes in these technologies and practices in terms of cost and capital requirements

5. *Entity structure:* organizational and capital structure common to most firms in the same industry.

6. *Normal performance:* average financial and other performance parameters for an organization in the industry of a particular size

7. *Noneconomic constraints:* legal regulations, financial reporting provisions, environmental restrictions, or other operative noneconomic constraints on industry activities; the important applicable traditions, beliefs, normal practices, and prevailing thought trends affecting the organization

General Conceptual Knowledge of Organizational Design   It has been this book's intention to acquaint the reader with some of the general conceptual understandings required to successfully execute an organizational design. This discussion of organizational design represents a review of the first five chapters of the book. It is logical for an individual or group studying organizational design to start by defining the envisioned organization. Recall that in Chapter One an organization was defined as a complex social unit that is deliberately designed to achieve some specific purpose and that has the following characteristics: a locus of power, division of labor, substitutability of personnel, and a history. Given this definition, it is fairly easy to discover the key elements, listed here, in any organization:

1. a goal or set of goals
2. some system to provide for a social unit
3. a scheme for distributing the power
4. a scheme for dividing labor, that is, a set of task definitions that describe the work to be done, how it is to be done, and how it is to be divided
5. provisions for the substitutability of personnel, that is, a set of role definitions that describe the functions of each of the information processors

6. a method for maintaining the history of the organization, that is, a way of recording the decisions made and the rules established for the organization

These components of every organization can be derived from a conceptual understanding of the characteristics of open systems and the nature of complexity. The major characteristics of open systems, which were discussed in Chapter Five, include: importation of energy and information from the environment, change of information from a given state to another, output of information and energy to the environment, the cyclic nature of information exchange, negative entropy, negative feedback loops, dynamic homeostasis, differentiation, integration, equifinality, and systems integrity. A basis for understanding the notion of complexity was developed in Chapter Six. The three basic causes of complexity are systems linkages, systems hierarchy, and systems spiral effects.

From the standpoint of general conceptual understanding, the designer needs to make provisions for the execution of the five functions performed in an organization: process following, problem solving, decision making, conflict management, and change management. (Chapters Eight and Nine gave detailed definitions of each of these five functions.)

Next, the designer must apply knowledge of the general concepts of organizational design to the selection of and interactions between the information processors within the system. This knowledge is derived from understanding the nature of the information and the information processors that are in the system (see Chapters Two and Three). The designer is concerned with understanding the amount, variety, and type of information present in the system, particularly the characteristics of the information flow—whether the flow is routine or nonroutine and whether the values of people in the organization are shared or dissimilar—since a large number of design decisions are based on these characteristics. In addition, there is concern for the selection and distortion characteristics of the organization's information processors. These characteristics limit the organization's performance and the interactions between the information processors in the organization.

Although the process of organizational design is creative, there are nevertheless these specific questions for the designer to consider:

1. What do I want the organizational outputs to be?

2. What inputs do I have or what inputs can I get to use in generating these outputs?

3. What tasks, functions, or transformations must be performed to get from inputs to outputs?

4. What tasks must be performed to maintain the system? (Remember that systems maintenance is required because all organizations are open systems.)

5. What information processors—conceptual, technical, and human—do I need to perform these tasks?

(These first five questions help to define the basic nature of the system and are shown in Figure 10-2.)

Figure 10-2

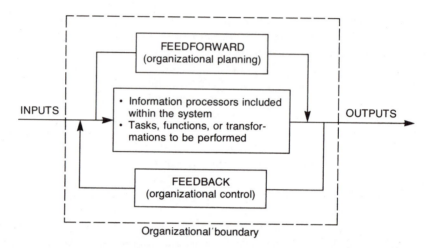

6. To what extent shall I attempt to standardize? This depends on the variety of routine information in the system. The more variety, the less standardization is possible. The designer's attempts at standardization consist of developing standard operating procedures to reduce the amount of uncertainty with which he or she must deal.

7. To what extent shall I attempt to specialize? This depends on the variety of information in the system. The more variety, the more specialization is required. (Remember, although standardization and specialization are related through their dependence on the same factor—the variety of information in the system—they are fundamentally different concepts.) This same question can also be posed in the following way: To what extent can I divide by function? For example, research and development, production, marketing, and accounting can represent the essential functions of some organizations and not of others.

8. How much fragmentation shall I have? This depends on the total amount of the information in the system. The more information, the greater the need to fragment or divide the task. Remember, fragmentation is related to the division of labor when the division is caused by the amount of work rather than the kind of work.

9. How much decentralization shall I have? This depends on the routineness of the information in the system. The more routine the information, the less decentralization is required. Remember, centralization refers to the distribution of power in the system. The closer power is to the actual execu-

tion of the task, the more decentralized the system. The further power is from the actual execution of the task, the more centralized the system. Be sure not to get fragmentation—the dividing of tasks—confused with decentralization—the dividing of power. The division of power is based on the amount of nonroutine information flowing at the actual execution of the task. The greater the amount of nonroutine information at a point, the greater the degree of decentralization. For example, a research and development department deals with a greater flow of nonroutine information than a production department. It consequently exhibits a greater degree of decentralization.

10.   What vertical relationships are required? This depends on the natural flow of information in the system, which is the flow required for task accomplishment. Remember that all systems are hierarchical and as such have a nesting relationship with other systems. Nested relationships are systems that are not only connected to but also integral parts of another system. This hierarchical set of relationships creates special problems of complexity for the manager. In order to relieve the pressure created by these relationships, the manager relies on reorganization.

11.   What horizontal relationships are required? This also depends on the natural flow of information in the system. In horizontal and vertical relationships, the direction of the natural flow of information is important, and artificial relationships that are not based on this task accomplishment should be avoided. Horizontal relationships depict systems elements that are linked together. The manager's problem is to understand why each link exists and what transactions take place at each link. These systems linkages create special problems of complexity for the manager. In order to relieve the complexity that links one system, or one element, to another, management utilizes buffers. Hierarchical relationships and systems linkages are both utilized to reduce the amount of nonroutine information with which society must deal.

12.   How can I structure the system to perform effectively within its task environment? To what extent should the system be closed or open? If the system is open, to what extent can the manager structure systems interfaces to deal with the environment; that is, how adaptable can the system be to its environment?

13.   How shall I design mechanisms to control the performance of the system? This question relates to the utilization of formal and informal feedback loops for purposes of systems control.

14.   How will the manager provide for planning mechanisms in the system? Which feedforward loops can the manager design and utilize to assist in the planning functions of the system?

(Questions 6 through 14 relate to the basic nature of systems. Questions 6 through 11 are related primarily to the design of the social system. Questions 12, 13, and 14 are specifically related to the control and planning functions of systems.)

15.   To what extent can I capture the organizational design in standard operating procedures? Remember that one of the key purposes of organizations is to make nonroutine systems more routine. One of the tests of whether this is accomplished is whether the organizational design can be captured in standard operating procedures. If only a very little can be, then it is likely that the design is ineffective.

(Question 15 differs from the first fourteen in that it is one measure of the overall success of the organizational design effort.)

The organization's design of standard operating procedures is its way of reducing complexity for society. Its success in this task is directly related to the degree that it makes the world more routine for individuals and groups. The designer must answer many questions as he proceeds in the design of the organizations. These fifteen questions constitute a general conceptual understanding of organizational design. The designer's knowledge of the general characteristics and traits of organizations will provide clues to the answer to each question. It should be understood that the questions are not completely independent of each other, but they are discrete enough to require individual attention.

Earlier, organizational design was compared with painting a picture or composing a song. This analogy is only partially correct because the design of an organization is never complete. There are three basic reasons why organizational design is a highly dynamic process:

1.   The other systems in the environment with which the organization must interact are always changing.
2.   The larger systems of which the organization is a subsystem are always changing.
3.   The subsystems (information processors) that make up the organization are always changing.

Change within the system and in its relationships with other systems, either vertical or horizontal, results in increased complexity for the system. This complexity must be managed by the organization if the organization is to survive.

Necessary Management Skills

The skills needed to maintain the operations of the organization are distinct from those needed for effective organizational design. Maintenance of operations requires management skills. Management, the process or activity of accomplishing a desired result through the intelligent use of organizational resources, represents a synthesis of the five principal organizational functions.

It is interesting to note the pattern with which the five organizational functions have been presented. The first three functions describe the organizational information flows in a static state:

1. *Process following:* Process following requires that a person follow the path of standard processes that employ routine information to obtain standard results.

2. *Problem solving:* Some problems are characterized by routine information flows and can be solved using standard information processors according to some standard operating procedure. Other problems are characterized by nonroutine information flows and require a different set of managerial strategies if satisfactory solutions are to be found. When faced with such problems, managers must discover ways to break their problem sets, to get out of their standard operating procedures so that they can see new relationships and get new understandings.

3. *Decision making:* Decision making is choosing between alternatives. We discussed three types of decision systems: bureaucratic decision systems, which are characterized by arrangements of standard information processes dealing with routine information; collegial decision systems, which are characterized by nonroutine continuous information situations; and political decisions systems, which are characterized by nonroutine discontinuous information situations.

To the extent that the organization can be isolated or closed, these three functions in the system are an adequate description of the firm. However, the organizations we encounter are open systems; there is no permanent state in which the organization can achieve its goals. The evolving environment creates the requirements for the fourth and fifth basic organizational functions:

4. *Conflict management:* Conflict is a breakdown in standard decision-making processes that causes organizations to have difficulty in selecting an action alternative. The organization's reactions to conflict include eliminating the conditions of conflict and competition, eliminating the causes of conflict, and conflict resolution (problem solving, persuasion, bargaining and "politics," and withdrawal). Attempts to eliminate the cause of conflict or reliance on a certain conflict resolution strategy mainly depend on whether the information is routine, nonroutine continuous, or nonroutine discontinuous.

5. *Change management:* Systems change is any modification that occurs in inputs or processes that causes the outputs of the system to be noticeably different from what it was before the modification. Systems change is of concern because we need to know how variations in inputs or processors affect outputs. The selection of a change strategy in which people are involved is partially determined by the extent to which the

information flows are routine, nonroutine continuous, or nonroutine discontinuous.

Each of our five organizational functions has three elements, one that deals with routine information and two that deal with nonroutine information (see Figure 10-3).

As we look at this analysis, we might suggest the following:

1. Given a routine information flow characterized by well-defined standard operating procedures, we might expect the decision system to be bureaucratic. Conflict would be primarily caused by a felt need for joint decision making. The most useful change strategy would be rational-empirical.

2. Given a nonroutine information flow without the presence of well-defined standard operating procedures, we would first identify the information flow as either continuous or discontinuous. Then we would look to other systems characteristics, namely, clarity of the value systems, specificity and agreement about goals, skill in bargaining and consensus making, selection and distortion characteristics of the information processors, and the ability and the willingness of the participants to control resource systems (wield power), if we are to be able to determine the type of decision system, the cause of conflict, and the most likely change strategy. If the information flow is continuous, then the decision system would probably be collegial, the conflict would likely be caused by differences in perception, and the most appropriate change strategies would likely be normative-reeducative. If the information flow is discontinuous, then the decision system would probably be political, the conflict cause would likely be differences in goals, and the most appropriate change strategies would likely be power-coercive. It should be understood that this analysis leads to the most likely match but *not* the only match. It should also be remembered that one of the key problems in the management of systems is that the skills required to deal with routine information flows are significantly different from those required for nonroutine continuous and discontinuous information flows.

Summary

In the last two chapters of the book we have attempted to show that describing the information flows within an organization provides a useful tool that facilitates understanding the organization. The information perspective is also intended for those with a desire for action. It specifies what information flows need to be created or eliminated to alter the organization's outputs.

Another major area stressed in Chapters Six and Seven is organization from the systems perspective. Figure 10-4 illustrates the basic systems con-

Figure 10-3

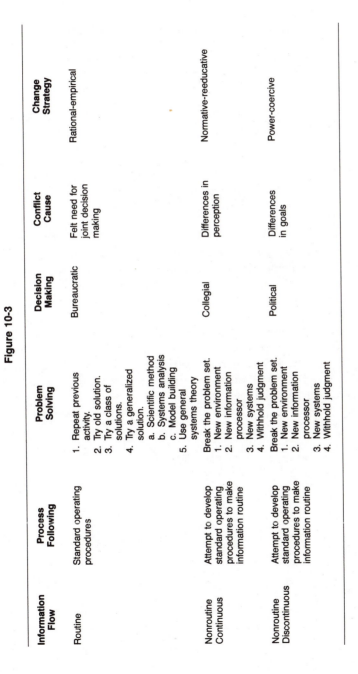

Information Flow	Process Following	Problem Solving	Decision Making	Conflict Cause	Change Strategy
Routine	Standard operating procedures	1. Repeat previous activity. 2. Try old solution. 3. Try a class of solutions. 4. Try a generalized solution. a. Scientific method b. Systems analysis c. Model building 5. Use general systems theory	Bureaucratic	Felt need for joint decision making	Rational-empirical
Nonroutine Continuous	Attempt to develop standard operating procedures to make information routine	Break the problem set. 1. New environment 2. New information processor 3. New systems 4. Withhold judgment	Collegial	Differences in perception	Normative-reeducative
Nonroutine Discontinuous	Attempt to develop standard operating procedures to make information routine	Break the problem set. 1. New environment 2. New information processor 3. New systems 4. Withhold judgment	Political	Differences in goals	Power-coercive

cepts: inputs, outputs, transformations, planning, control, and the organizational systems boundary.

Figure 10-4.   Basic Systems Concepts

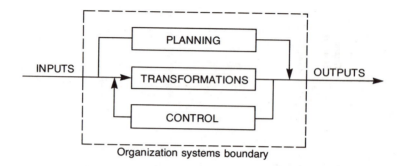

Information flows through the organization. Our understanding of organizations is assisted by looking at the basic systems concepts and the operation of the five basic organizational functions with the flows of routine and nonroutine information in the system. This book and its information perspective are intended to provide a framework that allows each reader to understand the organizations they encounter. Using the growing body of organizational theory knowledge, a person will be able to understand organizational processes and be able to manage organizations more effectively. One of the key resources utilized by managers is the organization itself. The information systems perspective permits the manager to utilize this resource more intelligently.

Bibliography

Ackoff, Russell L., Gupta, Shiv K., and Minas, J. Sayer. *Scientific Method: Optimizing Applied Research Decisions.* New York: Wiley, 1962.

Alexander, M. J. *Information Systems Analysis.* Chicago: Science Research Associates, 1974.

Allen, Thomas J. "Communications in the Research and Development Laboratory." In *Groups and Organizations: Integrated Readings in the Analysis of Social Behavior,* ed. Bernard L. Hinton and H. Joseph Reitz. Belmont, Calif.: Wadsworth, 1971.

Asch, S. E. "Effects of Group Pressure upon the Modification and Distortion of Judgements." In *Groups and Organizations: Integrated Readings in the Analysis of Social Behavior,* ed. Bernard L. Hinton and H. Joseph Reitz. Belmont, Calif.: Wadsworth, 1971.

Baker, Frank. "Introduction: Organizations as Open Systems." In *Organizational Systems: General Systems Approaches to Complex Organizations,* ed. Frank Baker. Homewood, Ill.: Irwin, 1973.

Blakeney, Roger N., Matteson, Michael T., and Domm, Donald R. "Classical and Instrumental Learning." In *The Individual and the Organization,* ed. Donald R. Domm, Roger N. Blakeney, Michael T. Matteson, and Robert Schofield. New York: Harper & Row, 1973.

Bobbitt, H. Randolph, Jr. *Organizational Behavior.* Englewood Cliffs, N.J.: Prentice-Hall, 1974.

Bowers, David G., and Seashore, Stanley E. "Predicting Organizational Effectiveness with a Four-Factor Theory of Leadership." In *Groups and Organizations: Integrated Readings in the Analysis of Social Behavior,* ed. Bernard L. Hinton and H. Joseph Reitz. Belmont, Calif.: Wadsworth, 1971.

Bruner, J. S. "Social Psychology and Perception." In *Readings in Social Psychology,* 3rd ed., ed. E. Maccoby et al. New York: Holt, Rinehart and Winston, 1958.

Bunker, Douglass R., and Dalton, Gene W. "The Comparative Effectiveness of Groups and Individuals in Solving Problems." In *Managing Group and Intergroup Relations,* ed. Jay W. Lorsch and Paul R. Lawrence. Homewood, Ill.: Irwin, 1972.

Carzo, Rocco, Jr., and Yanouzas, John N. *Formal Organization, A Systems Approach.* Homewood, Ill.: Irwin, 1967.

Chin, Robert, and Benne, Kenneth D. "General Strategies for Effecting Changes in Human Systems." In *The Planning of Change,* 2nd ed., ed. Warren G. Bennis, Kenneth D. Benne, and Robert Chin. New York: Holt, Rinehart and Winston, 1969.

"Chrysler Digs Itself an Economy Foxhole." *Business Week,* November 30, 1974, p. 24.

Clark, Frank J., Gale, Ronald, and Gray, Robert. *Business Systems and Data Processing Procedures.* Englewood Cliffs, N.J.: Prentice-Hall, 1972.

Cleland, David I., and King, William R., *Management: A Systems Approach.* New York: McGraw-Hill, 1972.

Cyert, Richard M., and March, James G. *A Behavioral Theory of the Firm.* Englewood Cliffs, N.J.: Prentice-Hall, 1963.

De Greene, Kenyon B. *Sociotechnical Systems: Factors in Analysis, Design and Management.* Englewood Cliffs, N.J.: Prentice-Hall, 1973.

Deutsch, Morton. "A Theory of Co-operation and Competition." *Human Relations,* 1949, *2,* 129–152.

Drever, James. *A Dictionary of Psychology,* rev. Harvey Wallerstein. Baltimore, Md.: Penguin, 1964.

Feibleman, J., and Friend, J. W. "The Structure and Function of Organization." In *Systems Thinking,* ed. F. E. Emery. Middlesex, England: Penguin, 1970.

Galbraith, Jay. *Designing Complex Organizations.* Menlo Park, Calif.: Addison-Wesley, 1973.

Galbraith, Jay. *Organization Design.* Reading, Mass.: Addison-Wesley, 1977.

Georgious, Petro. "The Goal Paradigm and Notes Toward a Counter Paradigm." *Administrative Science Quarterly,* 1973, *18,* 291–310.

Hammond, Leo Keith, and Goldman, Morton. "Competition and Non-Competition and Its Relationship to Individual and Group Productivity." In *Groups and Organizations: Integrated Readings in the Analysis of Social Behavior,* ed. Bernard L. Hinton and H. Joseph Reitz. Belmont, Calif.: Wadsworth, 1971.

Hinton, Bernard L., and Reitz, H. Joseph, eds. *Groups and Organizations: Integrated Readings in the Analysis of Social Behavior.* Belmont, Calif.: Wadsworth, 1971.

Hollander, Edwin P. *Principles and Methods of Social Psychology.* New York: Oxford University Press, 1967.

Hutchinson, Harry D. *Money, Banking, and the United States Economy,* 2nd ed. New York: Appleton-Century-Crofts, 1971.

Janis, Irving L. *Victims of Groupthink.* Boston: Houghton Mifflin, 1972.

Jelinek, Mariann. "Technology, Organizations, and Contingency." *Academy of Management Review,* 1977, 2, (1), 17–26.

Kaplan, Abraham. *The Conduct of Inquiry: Methodology for Behavioral Science.* San Francisco, Calif.: Chandler, 1964.

Katz, D., and Kahn, R. L. *The Social Psychology of Organizations.* New York: Wiley, 1966.

Keynes, John Maynard. *The General Theory of Employment, Interest and Money.* New York: Harcourt, Brace, 1936.

Leavitt, H. J. "Some Effects of Certain Communication Patterns on Group Performance." *Journal of Abnormal Social Psychology,* 1951, *46,* 38–50.

Lewen, Kurt. "Group Decision and Social Change." In *Readings in Social Psychology,* ed. T. M. Newcomb and E. L. Hartley. New York: Henry Holt and Co., 1947.

Litterer, Joseph A. *The Analysis of Organizations,* 2nd ed. New York: Wiley, 1973.

Lorsch, Jay W., and Lawrence, Paul R. *Organization Planning: Cases and Concepts.* Homewood, Ill.: Irwin, 1972.

March, James G., and Simon, Herbert A. *Organizations.* New York: Wiley, 1958.

"Members of the Wedding," *Forbes,* February 15, 1975, p. 33.

Miller, George A. "The Magical Number Seven, Plus or Minus Two: Some Limits on Our Capacity for Processing Information." *Psychological Review,* 1956, *63* (2), p. 95.

Mintzberg, Henry. *The Nature of Managerial Work.* New York: Harper & Row, 1973.

"The Mobil Offer That Won Marcor." *Business Week,* August 10, 1974, p. 45.

Moch, Michael K. "Structure and Organizational Resource Allocation." *Administrative Science Quarterly,* 1976, *21,* 661–674.

Mott, Paul E. *The Characteristics of Effective Organizations.* New York: Harper & Row, 1972.

Newman, William H., and Logan, James P. *Business Policies and Management.* 4th ed. Cincinnati, Ohio: South-Western, 1959.

"The Oil Companies Did Spectacularly Last Year. This Year? A Very Different Story." *Forbes,* January 1, 1975, pp. 216–219.

Perrow, Charles B. *Organizational Analysis: A Sociological View.* Belmont, Calif.: Brooks/Cole, 1970.

Peter, Laurence J., and Hull, Raymond. *The Peter Principle: Why Things Always Go Wrong.* New York: Morrow, 1969.

Reitz, H. Joseph. *Behavior in Organization.* Homewood, Ill.: Irwin, 1977.

Sauvain, Harry. *Investment Management,* 4th ed. Englewood Cliffs, N.J.: Prentice-Hall, 1973.

"Selling Business a Theory of Economies." *Business Week,* September 8, 1973, p. 85.

"Shipping: A Supertanker Glut Hurts the Market." *Business Week,* November 8, 1974, p. 63.

Simon, Herbert A. *Administrative Behavior.* New York: Macmillan, 1945.

Steiner, George A. and John B. Miner. *Management Policy and Strategy.* New York: Macmillan, 1977.

Stoner, J. A. F. "Risky and Cautious Shifts in Group Decision: The Influence of Widely-Held Values." *Journal of Experimental Social Psychology,* 1968, *4,* 442–459.

Summers, Edward L., and Knight, Kenneth E. *Management Advisory Services by CPA's, a Study of Required Knowledge.* New York: American Institute of Certified Public Accountants, 1976.

Toffler, Alvin. *Future Shock.* New York: Random House, 1970, chap. 7.

Vancil, Richard F. "Strategy Formulation in Complex Organizations." *Sloan Management Review,* 1976, *17,* 1–18.

Van Gigch, John P. *Applied General Systems Theory.* New York: Harper & Row, 1974.

Voich, Dan, Jr., et al. *Information Systems for Operations and Management.* Cincinnati, Ohio: South-Western, 1975.

Vroom, Victor H. *Work and Motivation.* New York: Wiley, 1964.

Woodward, J. *Industrial Organization: Theory and Practice.* London: Oxford University Press, 1965.

Index